Defeat in Malaya: the fall of Singapore

Defeat in Malaya

the fall of Singapore

Arthur Swinson

Editor-in-Chief: Barrie Pitt
Art Director: Peter Dunbar

Military Consultant: Sir Basil Liddell Hart
Picture Editor: Bobby Hunt

Executive Editor: David Mason
Designer: Sarah Kingham
Cover: Denis Piper
Research Assistant: Yvonne Marsh
Cartographer: Richard Natkiel
Special Drawings: John Batchelor

Photographs for this book were especially selected from the following Archives: from left to right page
2-3 Keystone Tokyo; 9 Keystone Tokyo; 10 Imperial War Museum; 11 Australian War Memorial; 12-13
Associated Press; 14 Imperial War Museum; 15 Associated Press; 16 US National Archives/Keystone Tokyo;
17 US Navy; 19 Popperfoto/A J Barker/Australian War Memorial; 20 Keystone Tokyo; 22 IWM; 24-25 The
Mansell Collection; 27 Popperfoto; 28 Popperfoto; 29 Popperfoto; 30 Radio Times Hulton Picture Library;
32-33 IWM; 34 Radio Times Hulton Picture Library; 34-35 Blackstar; 36 Blackstar/IWM; 37 IWM/Australian
War Memorial; 38 IWM; 39 IWM; 40-41 Blackstar; 42-43 Australian War Memorial; 44 IWM; 45 IWM; 46 IWM;
47 IWM; 46-47 IWM; 49 Keystone Tokyo; 52 IWM; 53 Keystone; 54 Lady Heath/IWM; 56-57 IWM; 58-59 IWM;
60 Popperfoto; 61 IWM; 63 IWM; 64 IWM; 64-65 IWM; 66 IWM; 68-69 IWM; 68 IWM; 72-73 Keystone Tokyo;
74-75 IWM; 76-77 IWM; 78-79 IWM; 80 Australian War Memorial; 83 IWM; 84 IWM; 87 IWM; 89 IWM; 90 Air
Ministry; 91 Air Ministry; 92 Keystone Tokyo; 94-95 Keystone; 94 Keystone; 95 Keystone Tokyo; 96-97
Keystone Tokyo; 98-99 IWM; 100-101 Australian War Memorial; 103 IWM; 104 Keystone Tokyo; 105 Keystone
Tokyo; 108-109 Australian War Memorial; 110 Keystone; 111 IWM; 110-111 Keystone; 112 IWM; 112-113 IWM;
113 IWM; 114-115 Australian War Memorial; 116 Australian War Memorial; 118-119 IWM; 122-123 Australian
War Memorial; 126-127 Australian War Memorial; 127 Australian War Memorial; 128-129 Keystone; 130-131
Australian War Memorial; 132-133 IWM; 134 IWM; 135 IWM; 136 Air Ministry; 137 Air Ministry; 138 Popperfoto;
142-143 US Navy; 144 Australian War Memorial; 145 Keystone Tokyo; 146-147 IWM; 148 Keystone; 151 Keystone;
152-153 IWM; 154-155 Keystone Tokyo; 156 IWM; 167 IWM; 158-159 Popperfoto.

First printing: January, 1970
Second printing: September, 1970
Printed in United States of America

Ballantine Books Inc.
101 Fifth Avenue, New York, NY10003
An Intext Publisher

Contents

Collapse of a facade

Introduction by Captain Sir Basil Liddell Hart

Arthur Swinson's book is an able and fascinating account of the Japanese campaign in Malaya which was launched in December 1941 and culminated in the fall of Singapore, early in February 1942.

In the Japanese plan, the task of conquering Malaya and Singapore was allotted to General Yamashita's Twenty-fifth Army, comprising three divisions with supporting troops – a combat strength of about 70,000, and a total strength of about 110,000. Moreover the sea-transports available only sufficed to carry a quarter of the force direct across the Gulf of Siam – 17,000 combat troops, and 26,000 in all. This advanced fraction was to seize the northern airfields. The bulk of Yamashita's army was to move overland, from Indo-China through Siam.

The chief Japanese landings were made at Singora and Patani on the Siamese neck of the Malay Peninsula, with four subsidiary landings further north on the coast of Siam. These landings were made in the early hours of 8th December, by local time. The intended British forestalling advance, Operation 'Matador', started too late because of reluctance to cross the frontier before Siam's neutrality had been violated by the Japanese. By the morning of 10th December the Japanese 5th Division had already swung across to the west coast and penetrated the frontier of Malaya, advancing by two roads into Kedah.

That day a decisive disaster befell the British at sea. After the decision in July to cut off Japan's oil supplies, Winston Churchill had 'realised the formidable effects of the embargoes' – belatedly, by his own admission – and a month later, on 25th August, proposed the dispatch of what he called a 'deterrent' naval force to the East. Accordingly the *Prince of Wales* and the battle-cruiser *Repulse* sailed for Singapore – but without any aircraft carrier. The one that had been earmarked ran ashore in Jamaica and had to be docked for repairs. There was another actually in the Indian Ocean, and within reach of Singapore, but no orders were given for her to move there.

The *Prince of Wales* and *Repulse* reached Singapore on 2nd December, and next day Admiral Sir Tom Phillips arrived to take command of the 'Far Eastern Fleet'. By midday on the 8th Phillips heard that they were disembarking their troops at Singora and Kota Bahru, while covered by at least one battleship of the *Kongo* class, five cruisers and twenty destroyers. In the late afternoon Phillips gallantly sailed north with what was called Force Z – his two big ships and an escort of four destroyers – to strike at the transports, although no shore-based air cover could be provided so far north now that the airfields there were lost.

In the evening of the 9th the weather cleared, and with it his cloak of obscurity. His Force Z was spotted from the air. So he turned south and headed for Singapore. But that night a signal came from there reporting, mistakenly, that a Japanese landing had been made at Kuantan, a midway point. Reckoning that surprise might be possible, and the risk justified, he altered course for Kuantan.

The Japanese were well prepared for any interception move by Force Z, whose arrival at Singapore had been broadcast to the world. Their elite 22nd Air Flotilla, with the best pilots of the Naval Air Arm, was based on the airfields near Saigon, in the south of Indo-China. Both ships were sunk, the *Repulse* by 1230 and the *Prince of Wales* by 1320.

This stroke settled the fate of Malaya – and Singapore. The Japanese were able to continue their landings unchecked, and establish air bases ashore. The superiority of their air force over the meagre British air strength in Malaya was decisive in crumbling the resistance of the British troops and enabling their own troops to push down the Malay Peninsula and force the backdoor into Singapore.

From 10th December onwards, the British retreat down the west coast became almost continuous. Road blocks were overcome either by Japanese tanks and artillery or by flank threat from Japanese infantry infiltrating through the bordering jungle.

On the night of Sunday 8th February, 1942, the two leading divisions of the Japanese invading force, which had swept down the 500-mile length of the Malay Peninsula, crossed the narrow channel which separated Singapore island from the mainland. The crossing was made on an eight-mile stretch of the thirty-mile straits, which here were less than a mile in width.

Armoured landing craft carried the first waves of attackers, but the rest followed in any sort of boats that could be collected, and a number of the Japanese even swam across – with their rifles and ammunition. Some of the craft were sunk, but most of the assault troops landed safely, helped by failures on the defenders' side that have never been satisfactorily explained. The beach searchlights were not exposed, means of communication failed or were not used, and the artillery was slow to put down its intended curtain of defensive fire.

By daylight 13,000 Japanese were ashore, and the defenders had fallen back to inland positions. Before midday the invaders' strength had risen to more than 20,000, and they had established a deep lodgement in the north-western part of the island – which is about the same size as the Isle of Wight. Later a third Japanese division landed, making the total well over 30,000.

There were two more divisions close behind on the mainland, but General Yamashita did not consider that he could effectively deploy them in the island advance.

Numerically, the defenders had more than sufficient strength in the island to repel the invasion, particularly as it came in the sector where it was most expected. General Percival, even now, had some 85,000 troops under his command – mainly British, Australian and Indian, with some local Malay and Chinese units. But the majority were ill-trained to match the Japanese attacking force, which was composed of troops specially selected for the purpose, and had been repeatedly outmanoeuvred in the dense jungle country or rubber plantations. The leadership in general was poor.

The air force had been outnumbered and outclassed from the outset of the campaign, and the little that remained was withdrawn in the final stage. Lack of protection against the enemy's fierce and incessant air attacks was the more demoralising to troops whose spirits were already depressed by the long retreat down the Malay Peninsula.

At Singapore the end came on Sunday 15th February – exactly a week after the Japanese landings. By that time the defenders had been driven back to the suburbs of Singapore city, which lies on the south coast of the island. Food stocks were running low and the water supply was liable to be cut off at any moment. That evening General Percival went out under a white flag to capitulate to the Japanese commander.

The immediate strategic effects of the loss of Singapore were disastrous, for it was quickly followed by the conquest of Burma and the Dutch East Indies – a two-pronged sweep that brought the Japanese menacingly close to India on the one flank and Australia on the other. Nearly four years of struggle followed, at immense cost, before Singapore was recovered as a result of Japan's own eventual collapse from exhaustion, and atomic bombshock.

But the longer and wider effects of Singapore's initial fall were beyond repair. Singapore had been a symbol – the outstanding symbol of Western power in the Far East, because that power had been erected and long maintained on British seapower.

The General and the task

On the morning of 2nd November 1941, three senior lieutenant-generals of the Imperial Japanese Army reported to the Chief of the General Staff, General Sugiyama. They were Masaharu Homma, Hitoshi Imamura, and Tomoyuki Yamashita, and the news they received was probably the most important in their whole careers: that in a few weeks' time Japan would be at war and they would be the chief field commanders. Homma would lead Fourteenth Army against General Douglas MacArthur in the Philippines; Imamura, Twenty-sixth Army against the Dutch East Indies; and Yamashita, Twenty-fifth Army against Malaya and Singapore. Pausing a moment to allow the generals to express their humble gratitude at the honour being paid them, Sugiyama was surprised to find himself under a barrage of questions from Homma, who wanted to know exactly who had compiled Intelligence summaries regarding enemy forces, who had laid down the target dates for completing the campaigns, and how troops for the operations had been allocated. Homma detested Sugiyama, and

before long the atmosphere had grown somewhat tense but fortunately Imamura was able to restore calm by pointing out that while target dates were necessary, no one was being asked to give guarantees. Homma, he added, should accept the task allotted to him and do his best. No soldier could do more.

In due course the meeting broke up and, having wished each other luck, Homma, Imamura and Yamashita departed for their respective headquarters to begin planning. Time was short and there was a great deal to do. Though appreciating Homma's viewpoint, it would not have occurred to Yamashita to argue in such a manner, for he was far too deeply versed in the *samurai* code which demanded that a soldier should carry out any task to the death, even if it were quite hopeless. His standards were rigid and absolute, as was his devotion to the Emperor.

Nevertheless, Yamashita received his command with mixed feelings, for

Lieutenant-General Tomoyuki Yamashita, Commander 25th Army

he knew that Tojo, Sugiyama and the Control Faction – one of the Japanese army political cliques – who now held power, had no love for him. He knew also that he would be closely watched and spied on, and any failure would be punished by dismissal and ignominy. Nor was he confident that success would bring any great rewards. Yamashita was a curious and complex character. At this time fifty-six years of age he was fat but highly strung, talented but often misguided, ruthless but fastidious, modern in many ways but shackled to the past. Though his mind cut through hypocrisy and evasion and, so far as soldiering was concerned, showed great realism and judgement, still his career suffered from divided loyalties and unresolved problems. At times he had been up to his neck in political adventure and his hands were far from clean. But even his enemies acknowledged his outstanding qualities of grasp and leadership, and his friends – especially young officers who had served on his staff – considered him the finest commander in the entire army. They had no doubts whatever that he would take Singapore.

He was born in the village of Osugi Mura on Shikoku, the smallest of Japan's main islands, and was the son of a doctor. For a time Yamashita had medical ambitions also, but his academic record was far from good and his parents eventually decided that his best hope lay in the army. Of their decision he said later: 'It was perhaps my destiny. I did not choose this career. Perhaps my father suggested the idea because I was big and healthy, and my mother did not seriously object because she believed, bless her soul, that I would never pass the highly competitive entrance examination.' However, he passed with ease and so entered the Military Academy at Hiroshima, passing out in 1908 with honours. Gazetted to the Infantry, he began learning his trade and made sufficient progress to earn a place at the Staff College. In 1916 he graduated in sixth place, then began a tour of duty on the General Staff. Here his qualities began to make themselves felt, and in three years he was promoted from captain to lieutenant-colonel. In 1919 he went to Switzerland

as military attaché; in 1926, as a major-general, he returned to instruct at the Staff College and then was posted to Vienna. Though he had married the daughter of General Nagayama in 1916, he had no children, and when away from duty his hobbies were fishing and gardening. He enjoyed music but disliked dancing; he did not own a car and never learned to drive. He was a deeply religious man, believing implicitly in the great God Norito, and the bad God or Devil, Susano, though whether he was so deeply attached to religion as to the *samurai* code may still be argued.

By the late 1920s the military cliques were in action in Japan, each protesting its patriotism and loyalty to the Emperor, but each ruthlessly ambitious and determined to get its way, no matter what the cost. Yamashita attached himself to the Imperial Way and its leader, the fanatical General Araki, who preached the need for military government. Yamashita had long detested the rich manufacturers who bought power, and mistrusted their political ambitions; and

he encouraged some of his young officers in their dangerous intrigues. While Yamashita was commanding 3rd Regiment, Tojo was commanding the 1st, and making this a centre of activity for a rival military clique, the Control Faction. They had already served together in Switzerland and disliked each other, and now political rivalry was to make them bitter enemies. In 1936, after the moderates had triumphed in the elections for the Diet, the War Ministry gave notice that the 1st Infantry Division (including the 1st and 3rd Regiments) would move to Manchuria. This provoked a ferment among the young officers, and two of Yamashita's proteges, Captain Ando and Captain Nonaka, came to him clutching the draft of a manifesto. This declared openly that war against Russia, China, Britain and the United States was not far away, and went on: 'We are persuaded that it is our duty to remove the villains who surround the throne. We, the children of our dear land of the gods, act with pure sincerity of heart.' Neither advising nor restraining the

Left: General Sugiyama, Chief of the Japanese General Staff. *Above:* Berlin, February 1941: Yamashita presents sword to Field-Marshal Brauchitsch

conspirators, Yamashita handed back the manifesto without comment, and on 26th February they went into action. Several members of the government were assassinated and life in Tokyo was brought to a halt. Yamashita found himself deputed to act as a negotiator between the government and the rebels, and on 28th conveyed the orders of the Emperor that everyone should lay down their arms and return to barracks. When Ando, Nonaka, and the group of young officers around them asked him what they should do he replied shortly, 'Kill yourselves – commit *seppuku*.' Most agreed, but when Captain Isobe declared that he had no intention of dying, Yamashita gave him a cold look of contempt and walked away. In his view, the *samurai* code demanded that failure should be atoned for by committing suicide and there could be no exceptions. At the same time, while encouraging the revolt in every conceivable manner, Yamashita had carefully done nothing which would implicate himself. One of the conspirators described his attitude as being 'between clever and cunning', and there was a good deal of truth in this. He was not cunning enough to deceive the Emperor and, after Araki and other senior officers had either been retired or dismissed from their posts, Yamashita found his own name removed from the promotion lists and he was sent to command a brigade in Korea. Here he did well, and later was sent to China, where he commanded a division. Afterwards he became Chief of Staff to the Northern China Army. Officers serving under him at this time heard him say more than once that he longed to die in action, so keenly did he feel the Emperor's reproof. But chances for active service were limited, and when the ban on promotion was lifted in 1937, he became a lieutenant-general. Steadily his military reputation grew and in July 1940 he was recalled to Tokyo, where he succeeded Tojo as Inspector-General Army Aviation. A few months later, however, when Tojo became War Minister, he was sent on a tour of Germany and Italy. At all costs, Tojo decided, he must be denied the chance of becoming a focus for dissident elements. Yamashita spent six months in Europe, touring depots and training establishments and studying the latest weapons of the German army. In his report he warned Tokyo that unless the Japanese army carried out an immediate modernisation programme of its air force, tanks, signals equipment and engineering techniques, it could not fight a modern war. Tojo was displeased with the report and for the most part ignored it. Yamashita on his return was despatched to the unimportant post of commander of the Kwantung Defence Army in Manchuria. Here he remained until November 1941 when he received orders from Sugiyama to report to Imperial Headquarters in Tokyo, and learned of his appointment to Twenty-fifth Army.

1937: Japanese infantry advance across the plains of Manchuria between Kanjurmiao and Changchumiao

Though not such a rabid imperialist as some, there can be no doubt that Yamashita looked on the coming war as just and inevitable. Later he wrote: 'The cause of this war is fundamentally economic. Fifty years ago Japan was more or less self-sufficient – the people could live off the land. Since then the population has almost doubled, so that Japan had to rely on outside sources for food supply and other economic requirements. In order to buy or import her commodities, she had to pay ultimately in commodities. This effort on her part was

prevented for one reason or another by other countries. Japan made attempts to solve the misunderstandings through peaceful methods, but when all her efforts were thwarted or negated she felt it necessary to engage in open warfare.'

This argument is, of course, quite specious and virtually amounts to a claim that if a country requires territory for economic reasons, this may be grabbed by force.

The truth was that the Japanese army had been intent on war for many years and gradually wrested power to pursue its aims. Even as far back as 1919 the American, Senator Henry Cabot Lodge, had warned:

'Japan is steeped in German ideas and regards war as an industry because from war she has secured all the extensions of the Empire. She will threaten the safety of the world.'

It was some while before the Senator's prophecies came to be realised, but in 1931 Japan invaded Manchuria and set up the Army State of Manchukuo. In 1937 she engineered the Peking incident, which sparked off war with China, and two

1937: the Japanese extend their hold over China. *Above:* Cavalry go into action.
Below: Landing party in Shanghai. *Right:* The occupation of Peking

Araki, War Minister, 1936, and fanatical leader of the Imperial Way

Hideki Tojo, Prime Minister, who led Japan to war

years later she carried the war into southern China. In September 1940, just before signing the Tripartite Pact with Germany and Italy, her troops went into northern Indo-China. These conquests had naturally aroused great opposition among the Western Powers, especially in the United States, where there were strong links with China. From 1938 the American Government had been operating an embargo on the export of manufactured goods and in the following two years the extent of this was widened until it included those commodities which Japan needed most of all: scrap iron and oil. By the summer of 1941 the strangle-hold was so effective that the Japanese leaders realised that they must submit to American demands and withdraw from their conquered territories, or fight. Not unexpectedly they chose to fight.

The step, however, which had made war inevitable – if it had not been already – was the elevation of Hideki Tojo to the post of prime minister. A sinister figure, he had made his reputation in 1937 as Chief of Staff of the Kwantung Army. Undisputed leader of the Control Faction, he had previously been head of the *kempei* or Military Police, which under his guidance had developed enormous powers throughout both the army and navy, and indeed the country at large. As War Minister he steadily increased both his own powers and the army's grip on the fate of the nation. Though, when he accepted the invitation to form a cabinet in October 1941, it was to avert a political crisis, he let his willingness to lead the nation in war be known. So the army and navy accelerated their preparations and the finalisation of war plans became a matter of great urgency.

Already these plans were far advanced. On 6th September an Imperial Conference had been held before the Emperor and a time limit was set on negotiations with America. Despite the Emperor's sternly expressed views that all diplomatic efforts must be exhausted before any other course was considered, requisition orders were placed for 400,000 tons of shipping, for the deployment of four million troops and the conscription of thousands of others. At the same time, an attack against Russia lobbied by one set of generals ('the Northwarders') was decisively rejected in favour of an attack against Siam, Malaya and the Philippines. Furthermore, Admiral Namamoto, Commander-in-Chief of the Combined Sea and Air Forces, who had fought against the plan to attack America and Britain, was worsted and denigrated as a defeatist. The Naval General Staff now allied itself with the army.

Masanobu Tsuji, Japan's expert on jungle warfare

Vice-Admiral Ozawa, Combined Force Commander

There were, however, important differences over the tactics to be employed against Malaya, and these were thrashed out at a series of inter-service conferences. The navy wanted the landings to be prefaced by a pro-longed bombardment of the beach defences and an intensive attack against air bases. Unless this were carried out, the Naval Staff argued, their warships would be vulnerable to air attack, and, as one officer put it, 'Tethered there guarding the convoys, we should be like sitting ducks.' The army on the other hand advocated the use of surprise. The generals were convinced that the British would not move a finger before war was declared or hostilities had commenced, by which time the assault troops would be ashore. Also, from first light 3rd Air Division would be in action and, with its great superiority in numbers and quality, should be able to attain air superiority within a few hours.

There were other factors involved in the argument. Dr Nishimura, the meteorological officer on Formosa, gave his views that on 6th and 7th December there would be moderate winds, but on the 8th the north-east monsoon would spring up, and from then on the sea along the Malayan seaboard would become increasingly choppy. The 8th December, therefore, was the last possible day for the

landings, and if time were spent on a preliminary bombardment, then the whole operation might end as a fiasco. It was quite probable that the landings could not be attempted again until the following April.

But despite this and other arguments, the Naval Staff dug their toes in; the risks to their warships were unacceptable, they said, and a compromise must be reached. Then, in the face of an apparent impasse, Vice-Admiral Jisaburo Ozawa, now designated Combined Force Commander, rose and addressed the conference. He understood the army's desire to land quickly and without prior bombardment, he said. Their reasons were valid and should be accepted by Admiral Yamamoto and the Naval Staff. Then, to the amazement of the whole conference and the horror of the Admiral, he declared, 'I say that the Navy should accept the Army's proposal, even at the risk of anni-hilation.' The argument was over and the shape of the Malayan invasion plan was agreed.

All this happened, of course, before Yamashita's appointment, and on taking over on 5th November he discovered that his interests had been watched by General Iida. It is doubtful if Yamashita had any considerable knowledge of Malaya, though it had come up from time to time in staff exercises, and he could have no doubt as to its immense economic importance to Japan, faced as she was by the Allied embargo. Taken together with Britain's great naval base on the island of Singapore, it presented a prize of staggering wealth.

But how was it to be captured? As Yamashita was now to discover, the High Command had been tackling this problem for the past year. In January 1941 on the island of Formosa a small unit called 'The Taiwan Army Research Section' had been set up under a minor figure in the Control Faction and henchman of General Tojo, called Colonel Masanobu Tsuji. Tsuji was a bossy, interfering little man, detested throughout the army as a 'thruster' and known to have been employed by Tojo to spy on senior commanders. Nevertheless he had great powers of perception and assimilation which were now to serve him to good stead, for his brief was to examine the whole question of jungle warfare as it would be waged in Malaya and solve the problems it presented. So with ten research assistants he began probing swiftly and deeply. How should tactics be adapted for tropical and jungle warfare? What special clothes and equipment would be necessary? How would communications be maintained? How would such matters as sanitation, hygiene and care of wounded be dealt with? As Tsuji recorded, 'We pestered specialists from every quarter. We even used our siesta time for lectures, which were always eagerly attended . . . This unimpressive group was certainly at that time the supreme authority on tropical warfare.' By the spring of 1941 Tsuji was turning his thoughts to the final objective of the campaign, the naval base at Singapore, and, after interrogating officers from both the army and navy, set down his conclusions in these terms:

1. Singapore Fortress was solid and strong on its sea front but the rear facing Johore Province was practically defenceless.

2. Newspaper reports of RAF fighter strength were intentional propaganda, exaggerating the real strength.

3. The British army in Malaya numbered from five to six divisions, with a total strength of approximately 80,000. The proportion of European troops was probably less than fifty per cent.

Despite the spy network which Japan had maintained throughout the Far East for many years, Tsuji found that until recently precise topographical data had been lacking. Fortunately for him a Major Terundo Kunitake had been attached to the consulate in Singapore, and used his time in making a survey of roads, rivers and bridges. Along the main trunk road running from Singapore to the Siam border, he reported, there were no less than 250 bridges, many more than Tsuji had estimated from the small-scale and inaccurate maps at his disposal. As he appreciated at once, the longer it took to repair the bridges during the advance south, the longer the British would have to build up the landward defences of Singapore. So he recommended that an entire engineer regiment should be allocated to each of the infantry divisions engaged, and an additional regiment under direct control of the army commander. Estimates of the type and quantity of bridging equipment were also revised in the light of the information supplied by Major Kunitake, and the engineers were set to work rehearsing their role in the Formosan jungles.

Rapidly absorbing all this material on assuming command, Yamashita was quite confident that he could carry out the task before him. One of the things which impressed him was that the bulk of the troops facing him would be Indians who, he remarked, 'should make things very much easier for us.' The idea that any Asian troops could stand up to the Japanese in open battle seemed to him quite ludicrous. In fact, when offered five divisions for the campaign, he replied, 'No – four will be enough. And I shall only call on the fourth if I really need it.' The formations eventually selected were Lieutenant-General Takuro Matsui's 5th Division, Lieutenant-General Renya Mutaguchi's 18th Division and the Imperial Guards Division under Lieutenant-General Nishimura. Of these, the highly mechanised 5th Division, which had served in China, was easily the most experienced and Yamashita's

Japanese Divisional Commanders

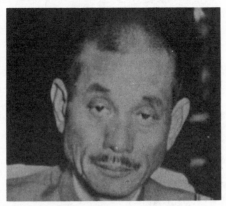

Matsui, 5th Division

Mataguchi, 18th Division

Nishimura, Imperial Guards Division

relations with its commander were excellent. His relations with Renya Mutaguchi, the choleric, ambitious commander of 18th Division were amicable too. They had both been stalwarts of the Imperial Way clique and in 1937 Mutaguchi had served as Yamashita's chief of staff. 18th Division, though not so highly mechanised or experienced as 5th Division, still enjoyed a sound reputation and would obviously do well under its present commander. On his arrival at Twenty-fifth headquarters, in fact, Mutaguchi had bustled in demanding a leading role for his formation and offering to lead the advance from the coast to Singapore. No one lusted more eagerly for military glory than Mutaguchi.

Relations with Takuma Nishimura, who commanded the Guards Division, were not so happy. He and Yamashita had clashed a few years earlier when Nishimura was president of a court-martial trying some young officers of the Imperial Way. The guardsman, who was both stubborn and of limited ability, resented being under Yamashita's command and resolved to obey his orders as little as possible. Though the Guards regiments were superb at ceremonial, they had done little field training and the Division had not been in action since the Russo - Japanese War of 1905. When Yamashita saw it on manoeuvres, he was somewhat horrified, and ordered Nishimura to lay on some intensive battle training at once. Nishimura, however, did nothing in this direction and when his division embarked for the campaign opinion among Twenty-fifth Army staff was that it was unfit for combat. To complicate matters further, Nishimura was an old ally of Field-Marshal Count Terauchi, Yamashita's superior at Southern Army who also had belonged to the Control Faction. Yamashita had enemies both above and below. He cannot have been happy to learn that Masanobu Tsuji was being thrust onto his staff as the personal spy of the prime minister, Tojo. It may be mentioned here that, when Yamashita decided to launch his offensive with three divisions instead of the five which were offered him, he did not do so out of bravado. In his view, the force selected was the largest which could be supplied as the

**Admiral Isoroko Yamamoto,
Commander-in-Chief of the
Imperial Japanese Navy**

line of communications lengthened
with the advance south to Singapore.
He had no faith whatsoever in any
headquarters run by Terauchi.

To complete the composition of
Yamashita's assault force, supporting
the infantry would be two regiments
of heavy field artillery and 3rd Tank
Brigade. Air cover would be provided
by 3rd Air Division which totalled
459 aircraft, and a further 159 aircraft
would be provided by the navy. Vice-
Admiral Ozawa's Southern Squadron,
which would be responsible for guarding the convoys till they reached the

Malayan coast, would comprise a
battle-cruiser, ten destroyers and five
submarines.

It was the second week in November
before Yamashita was able to leave
Tokyo and fly down to his headquarters. These were in the port of Samah,
on Hainan, a strategically placed
island which the Japanese had occupied in February 1939. It lies mid-way
between the south-eastern coast of
China and the coast of Indo-China.
Here Yamashita found feverish
activity and his staff were hurriedly
assembling – they had been drawn
from units and headquarters scattered
all over Japan and her occupied territories. Few of the officers knew each
other or had met Yamashita himself,

and how they would shake down as a team was a matter for speculation. Fortunately, however, Yamashita's personality made a deep and immediate impression, and haste, panic and confusion were avoided. The chief of staff was Lieutenant-Colonel Ichiji Sugita and there was also a deputy army commander, Major-General Managi.

So much for Twenty-fifth Army and its task. What was the plan? Briefly, this was that the invasion fleet would leave Samah on 4th December – four days before the outbreak of war – and split up into five convoys. Two of these, carrying Matsui's 5th Division and part of Mutaguchi's 18th Division would head for Singora, 120 miles north-west of the Thailand-Malayan border, in the Isthmus of Kra; two more convoys would head for Patani, sixty miles to the southeast; and a strong brigade group from 18th Division, under Major-General Takumo, would be transported to Kota Bharu on the Malayan coast, just south of the Thai border. As a glance at the map will show, the trunk roads through the Malayan peninsula run straight up to Singapore and Patani and so would facilitate communications along the axis of the advance. Also, as Yamashita could see at once, by using these Thailand ports, he would be able to get the bulk of his forces ashore before the British could cross the frontier from Malaya and oppose them. The landings at Kota Bharu would undoubtedly be opposed and the risks involved would be considerable. Nevertheless, Yamashita reasoned, it would constitute a useful diversion from the main thrust, and if all went well Takumi could make a swift dash inland to deal with the forward airfields. Everything depended on wresting air superiority from the start.

For the moment, however, there was the job of collecting the transports together, not only from Japanese ports but from Shanghai, Canton and Formosa. Lieutenant-Colonel Kera, Chief of Army Shipping, seemed confident that they would all show up before dark on 2nd December, the scheduled date but, in fact, by 1600 hours not a ship was in sight and Yamashita began wondering what had happened. Had the skippers misread their orders? Had Imperial Headquarters changed the plan without advising him? Or had Terauchi's headquarters made the first of many boobs? The situation became tense, for the embarkation schedule was a tight one, and unless troops and equipment could begin loading as planned, the result would be chaos. To complicate matters, there was a complete ban on radio signalling and a series of long distance telephone calls put through by the frantic Kera produced no information at all. The war, it seemed, or at least Yamashita's campaign, would begin with a fiasco. Then, just before sunset, some wisps of smoke were seen on the horizon and one by one the ships steamed into harbour. By noon the following day Yamashita was informed by his staff that embarkation had begun on schedule.

That evening he received final orders from Terauchi:
1. It is predetermined that military operations begin on the 8th December.
2. Twenty-fifth Army is to co-operate with the navy in the commencement of military operations for the occupation of Malaya.
3. Twenty-fifth Army will begin operations based on previous orders. However, if Japanese-American negotiations are concluded by the above fixed date, the military assault operations will be suspended.

No one seriously considered that operations would be called off, and some officers thought the insertion of an 'if' at this late stage might have a serious effect on morale. However, when Yamashita summoned his staff next morning to give out final instructions, confidence returned. Many officers had tears in their eyes and the occasion was charged with great emotion. For the Japanese, 8th December would be what 'Der Tag' had been for the Prussians in 1914. The day they had dreamed of and planned for so long; the supreme opportunity to smash the British and Americans and establish a new order in the Far East under the glorious sun of Japan. They had complete confidence in the campaign and in their commander. Nothing would stop them.

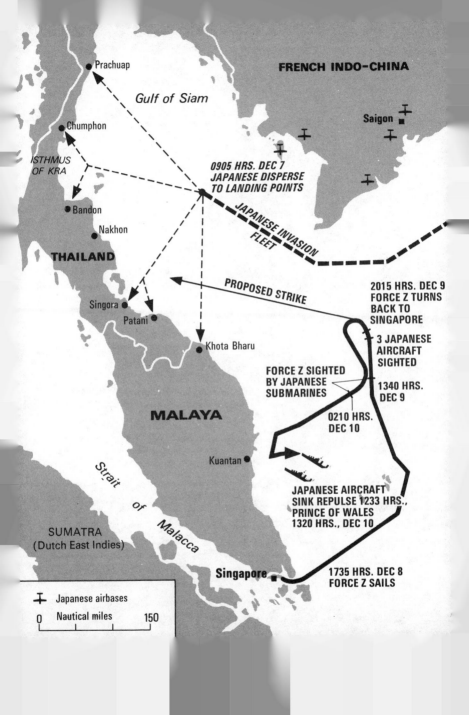

The fortress in the sun

'Here I am at Singapore, true to my word, and in the enjoyment of all the pleasure which a footing on such classic ground must inspire. This place possesses an excellent harbour . . . We are within a week's sail of China, close to Siam, and in the very seat of the Malayan Empire. Your station completely outflanks the Straits of Malacca and secures a passage for our China ships at all times, and in all circumstances . . .'

The writer was Sir Thomas Stamford Raffles and the year was 1819. With rivalry in the East Indies between the British and Dutch becoming more intense every year, Raffles (a servant of the East India Company) had been asked to go out and find a new port within the archipelago to form the centre of all native trade. Fortunately, before leaving Malaya the previous year, he had discovered the small island of Singapore, nestling close to the tip of the Malayan peninsula, and marked it down as a possible new post. Completely unknown to the Dutch, the place was mostly swamp and jungle and almost uninhabited. Raffles himself had come across it during the course of his Malayan studies, for many centuries previously there had been an ancient civilisation on the island, the ruins of which were still partly visible. Acting on Raffle's advice, the Company purchased Singapore from the Sultan of Johore and the British flag was hoisted there on 29th February 1819.

In shape Singapore island roughly resembles the Isle of Wight, extending some twenty-seven miles from east to west and thirteen miles (at its maximum width) from north to south. The Johore Strait which separates it from the mainland varies in width from 600 yards to 5,000 yards, and near the narrowest point the British built a causeway. The terrain is undulating, the only features of note being some hills near the centre of the island, including Bukit Timah and Bukit Mandai, which rise to 600 feet. In the south there is a low ridge called Pasir Panjang, about four miles in length, which overlooks the western approaches to the island. With the exception of the south-east, the coastline is broken by creeks and small rivers, lined with mangrove swamps. Most of the roads lead towards the town of Singapore, which lies on the southern shore, slightly towards the eastern end of the island. Here in 1941 lived some 550,000 people, divided like the population in Malaya itself into Chinese and Malays with a small proportion of Tamils and even fewer Europeans. If the site of Singapore was ideal, its climate was not. The island lies only ninety miles from the equator and the air is hot and humid. It is not a good climate and robs Europeans especially of both mental and physical energy. The climate, in fact, made a great impact on events between 1920 and 1941.

The Malayan peninsula is roughly 400 miles long and varies in width from 200 miles to 60; and as a glance at the map will show it runs from north to south with the Strait of Malacca on the west and the South China Sea on the east. It is joined to Thailand by the narrow neck of land called the Kra Isthmus. In size roughly comparable to England and Wales put together, Malay has a spine running down the centre, a ridge of jungle-covered hills rising to about 7,000 feet in the north and scaling down to 3,000 feet in the south. On either side of the hills lie coastal plains, flanked on the west coast by mangrove swamps and on the east by sandy beaches. The plains are cut by hundreds of rivers and streams making their way from the mountains to the sea, and, as these are often choked by thick jungle, there are large areas of swamp. Because of the heavy rainfall, (up to 260 inches in the mountains) vegetation grows luxuriously all the year round, and for the most part the Malayan jungles are far thicker than the Indian or the Burmese. There are giant trees and closely inter-weaved creepers, while at ground level the bushes are thick and seemingly impenetrable, and visibility may be no more than a yard or more. In the swampy areas there are thick belts of thorn bush, through which cutting a path is a slow, painful task. More than half the total area is covered with this dense, primeval jungle but on the western plain and in Johore large areas have been cleared for cultivation to a consider-

Malaya: paddy fields are planted

able depth, on either side of the road and railway. In the north there are rice-fields and in the south areas sown with tapioca and vegetables. Wherever cultivation is abandoned, if only for a short time, the jungle takes over again, and there is a secondary growth of quite incredible density and elephant grass up to six feet high.

In 1941 the population totalled between four and five million. Of these, two million were Malays, two million Chinese, and the rest Tamils from India. The European population totalled about 20,000. The Malays are a gentle race of fishermen and cultivators. They like to take life easily and would sit for hours under a palm until the coconuts drop, rather than climb up to pluck them. By contrast the Chinese, most of whom had come to Malaya to trade, showed tremendous energy and many had made sizeable fortunes. For the most part they seemed to lack political ambition and had no interest (up to the end of 1941, anyway) in the defence of the country. There were also several

thousand Japanese, many of them barbers or local photographers, though some owned rubber estates. It was a standing joke that a large proportion were in the pay of Japanese Intelligence.

The story of how the British took over Malaya is a tangled one which need not be told at length here. It was a process of founding trading posts, developing relationships with local rulers, and then signing treaties whereby Britain guaranteed protection in exchange for trading and other rights. By 1914, when the Sultan of Johore accepted a British Adviser, the country had gained a political structure which was to last till the arrival of the Japanese. This structure, though, was complex, and this complexity had its impact on events in the 1920s and 1930s. The British governor, for example, should he wish to reach a new agreement, would have to deal with no less than eleven separate governments. These represented the Straits Settlements of

Singapore, Malacca and Penang, which formed a British colony; the Federated States of Malaya (Perak, Selangor, Negri Semilan and Pahang); and the Unfederated States of Johore (Trengganu, Kelantan, Kedah, and Perlis). The last four states each had its own Sultan and was incorporated in the British Empire by separate treaty. Though this ram-shackle constitution might be just workable in times of peace, it was not designed to withstand the stresses of war. So far as most people were concerned, it would never have to.

Malaya to the British was not a bastion of imperial defence, but a gold mine – or to be more accurate a rubber and tin mine. Just after the turn of this century it had occurred to the British Government, that if only the right species of rubber plant could be found, the hold maintained by Brazil on world rubber supplies could be broken. So with the co-operation of the Royal Botanic Gardens, Kew, an envoy was sent to penetrate the forests of wild rubber

in Brazil and bring back specimens growing in soil and rainfall approximating to that found in Malaya. Eventually two species were selected, and large areas of jungle on the western plains of Malaya were cleared and then planted. The rubber trees took and the sap flowed freely. By 1941 the rubber estates covered no less than three million acres and produced over a third of the world's output, while the mines had been developed to such an extent that they were producing fifty-eight per cent of its tin.

This emphasis on the production of raw materials and on trade naturally made its impact on the European hierarchy and their scale of values. Businessmen considered themselves and their interests – including their pleasures – to be paramount. They rated themselves above administrators, and the interests of the armed forces barely entered their calculations at all. No commander, for example, dare march his troops through a rubber estate, even for

Rubber. *Right:* Draining latex from the trees. *Below:* Tappers bring in cans of latex for weighing

training which might be vitally necessary. This subjugation of defence interests is not so extraordinary as it may seem, for right through the 19th Century there had been no conceivable enemy. Until, under American pressure, Japan opened up her ports for international trade, she was sunk in primitive isolation, and afterwards Britain had regarded her as a friend. In 1902 the two countries signed a treaty of alliance.

It was 1915 before Japan gave the first hint to the world of her dreams of expansion, and in this year she published her 'Twenty-one Demands' on China. Though these were modified, after strong protests by Britain and America, she still gained important concessions in the Shantung peninsula and in southern Manchuria. For her help to the Allies in the First World War, she was granted a mandate over the Marianas, and the Caroline and Marshall Islands. More important, she began building up her navy which now became the third largest in the world. Then in 1929 came the Tanaka Memorial, a declaration of Japanese intentions which has sometimes been compared to Hitler's *Mein Kampf*. Baron Tanaka, who held the rank of general in the Japanese army, was prime minister and leader of the *Seiyukai* (Liberal) party, and in the Memorial set out his solution to Japan's problems:

'Japan's food supply and raw materials decrease in proportion to her population. If we merely hope to develop trade, we shall eventually be defeated by England and America, who possess unsurpassed capitalistic power. Our best policy lies in the direction of taking positive steps to secure rights and privileges in Manchuria and Mongolia. Having China's entire resources at our disposal, we shall proceed to conquer India, the Archipelago, Asia Minor, Central Asia and even Europe.'

In face of protests from the Western powers, the Japanese government dismissed the document as a forgery but events were soon to indicate that, as a statement of intentions it was only too accurate.

Count Tanaka, author of the notorious Tanaka Memorial

Eight years before the Memorial appeared, the British government had recognised that, with the elimination of the German navy and the rise of the Japanese navy, the world balance of naval power had swung from the Atlantic to the Pacific. The only British naval base in the Far East lay at Hong Kong, and this – apart from offering only limited facilities – could not be defended in time of war. So in 1921 the Committee of Imperial Defence examined the situation and recommended that a new base should be built at Singapore. On 16th June of that year Cabinet approval was given and the following year the exact site was chosen – on the northern side of the island, some five miles to the east of the causeway. Two years later, before the project had really got under way, the Labour government came into power and scrapped it. Fortunately, the life of this government was short, and upon their return to power, the Conservatives ordered that works should recommence. Also the question of defence was considered, and the army gave the firm opinion that an attack from the Malayan peninsula was almost impossible because of the terrain and the jungle. The only possible attack on Singapore, so the government was agreed, would be from the sea.

Now followed ten years of bickering between the services. The Air Ministry claimed that torpedo-bombers protected by fighters could, with the support of medium gun batteries, provide a cheaper and more efficient defence system than heavy gun batteries. The Admiralty and War Office, however, would have none of this, maintaining that heavy guns had always proved the strongest deterrent against warships. It was 1926 before the Committee of Imperial Defence came to a decision, and this was that the first stage of development should include close and medium batteries plus three 15-inch guns, and the question of aircraft versus heavy batteries should be decided later. More years were wasted in bickering and in 1929, when another Labour government took office, it decided to concentrate its efforts on disarmament. In 1930 a conference was held

Singapore Naval Base under construction: at the same time work on airfields was carried out

which resulted in the signing of the London Naval Treaty for the limitation and reduction of armaments. For Singapore a policy of go-slow was adopted.

By the following year this policy began to look somewhat misguided, for in Germany Hitler began his rise to power and the Japanese army, having staged an incident on the Southern Manchurian Railway, occupied Mukden and other strategic points and eventually gobbled up the whole of Manchuria. By this time the Chiefs of Staff were warning the government that 'it would be the height of folly to perpetuate our defenceless state in the Far East', and it was decided that plans for Singapore should be pushed ahead. But again inter-Service warfare broke out and it was May 1932 before the government gave its ruling that, while the gun should constitute the main weapon of defence, aircraft should provide valuable assistance.

The responsibility for the defence of Singapore would be shared by all three services which, it was hoped, would work in close collaboration.

But work went on very slowly and it was the end of 1935 – fifteen years after the initial decision to construct the base – that the first stage was completed. By then, the government had given permission for the installation of heavy gun batteries and a sense of urgency at last appeared. There was good cause for, apart from demanding parity in naval armaments, the Japanese were obviously aiming at the complete subjugation of China. Parallel with the construction of the naval base, work on airfields in Malaya went ahead, the main sites being selected at Kota Bharu and Kuantan. The reason for putting these so far north was the need for detecting enemy convoys as early as possible but the RAF disdained to consult the army, with the result that the airfields could not be defended against ground forces, once these had succeeded in landing. To add to the confusion, the defence scheme in operation at this time did

not include northern and eastern Malaya, so urgent revision was necessary.

Curiously enough, throughout all these years of bickering and indecision, it had occurred to barely anyone that Malay had over 1,000 miles of coastline, half of it exposed to Japanese attack. It had occurred to no one either that the defence of the naval base on Singapore island was bound up with the defence of the whole Malayan Peninsula. In 1937, however, a faint light of reality began penetrating the fog, and Major-General W G S Dobbie, GOC Malaya, was asked to look at the defence problem afresh and from the Japanese viewpoint. All his calculations were to be based on the assumption that a British Fleet could not arrive in under seventy days to carry out relief. Dobbie, a man of ability and great religious faith (he was to earn great distinction in the defence of Malta), began by carrying out a number of exercises with troops, and in October reported that, contrary to the orthodox view, landings by the Japanese on the eastern seaboard were possible during the north-east monsoon from October to March, and indeed this period was particularly dangerous because bad visibility would limit air reconnaissance. Dobbie also pointed out that, as a preliminary to their attack, the Japanese would probably establish advanced air bases in Siam, and might also carry out landings along the coast of that country. The main landing places, he predicted with extraordinary accuracy would be Singora and Patani in Siam, and Kota Bharu in Malaya. If this appreciaion were accepted, he urged, large reinforcements should be sent without delay. The appreciation was ignored. In July 1938, when Japanese ambitions had shown themselves in an even clearer light, Dobbie warned that the jungle in Johore (in southern Malaya) was not impassable to infantry, but again he was ignored. By 1939 all he had been able to wring out of the government was a paltry £60,000, most of which was spent on building machine gun emplacements along the southern shore of Singapore island and in Johore.

Left: General Dobbie: his warnings were ignored by the Government.
Above: Singapore volunteers prepare to go on training

Meanwhile, as the Japanese triggered off the Peking incident in July 1937, which led to war in north China, and then the following year landed troops in Amoy, some 300 miles northeast of Hong Kong, the Chiefs of Staff kept reviewing the Far East defences, and were urged by New Zealand to send a fleet at once and before the outbreak of hostilities. But attention was increasingly focused on Europe where Hitler was making ugly threats, and the ludicrous figure of Mr Neville Chamberlain was scurrying to and fro between London and Germany. In February 1939, the Chiefs of Staff completed yet another appreciation, based on the promise that the main enemies would be Germany, Italy and Japan. By now it was accepted that a fleet must be sent to the Far East, though its strength would have 'to depend on our reserves and the state of the war in the European theatre.' With the German situation fast dete-

riorating, no specific action was taken, however, and in May when the Committee of Imperial Defence held its session, though Japan was now rated a more serious enemy than Italy, the view was held that with so many unknown factors to be allowed for, 'it is not possible to state definitely how soon after Japanese intervention a Fleet could be despatched to the Far East.' Nor could the Committee, on its own confession, state even yet how many ships could be spared. By July it was decided to investigate the possibility of building up food stocks in Malaya for both civilians and troops to cover a period of six months. And just before Hitler marched into Poland, an Indian Brigade Group, a mountain artillery regiment and two bomber squadrons were sent out from India.

What then was the total strength available to defend the country now that war had become a reality? Incredibly the defence of northern Malaya was left in the hands of the Federated Malay States Volunteers, and of Johore to its States forces. The newly arrived Indian brigade

was held as a reserve for the defence of Johore. And Singapore island – which, it will be recalled, is over twenty miles in length – was entrusted to five regular battalions, two volunteer battalions, two coastal artillery regiments, three anti-aircraft regiments and four engineer fortress companies. There was an even smaller force at Penang. The six air force squadrons had a total of fifty-eight aircraft. If Japan attacked now only a token resistance could be offered.

It cannot be said that the situation greatly concerned the majority of people. In general the Malays were concerned only with events in their own *kampongs*, the Chinese attended to their business, and the Tamil labourers, mostly illiterate, were intent as always on survival. The British merchants and administrators remained blissfully unaware of the strategic situation and concentrated their energies chiefly on implementing government instructions to raise output of rubber and tin. These commodities were vital to the Allied war effort and demands would intensify with every month that

The last days of peace. *Above:* Indian troops on a training march. *Below:* Gurkhas move through thick jungle

Above: Reinforcements prepare to disembark at Singapore. *Below:* British, Australian and Dutch airmen on a forward airfield

Sir Shenton Thomas, the Governor
of the Straits Settlement

Air Chief Marshal Sir Robert
Brooke-Popham, C-in-C Far East

went by. Apart from marginal
changes, it cannot be said that life
in the European communities changed
very much. There was still whisky
at the club and the tennis courts
and golf links remained as immacu-
lately groomed as ever. Evening dress
was *de rigueur* for even minor social
occasions, and servants were cheap
and plentiful. From Malaya the war
seemed very, very far away and the
newsreels had an air of complete unreality. They would continue to do
so, even when Poland fell, and then
France, and when Hitler turned the
full fury of the German army and
air force against the people of Russia.

In 1940 the Governor of the Straits
Settlement was Sir Shenton Thomas,
the son of a Cambridge vicar, whose
experience had been gained in the
colonial service in Africa. In his six-
ties, he was finding the climate of
Singapore somewhat of a trial and
normally would have retired. Though
not without ability, he was not the
man for a crisis; he could not dominate events. Now he was in conflict
with the recently arrived GOC,
Lieutenant-General Bond, who was
horrified at the absence of defences
on Singapore and wanted to recruit a
coolie labour force to get things
moving. Thomas would not agree to
this and reported to the government
that: 'I conceive it to be our duty to
give absolute priority to the claims
of industry.' The government, so far
as one can tell, did not disabuse him
and the Chinese, Tamils and Malays
went on labouring in the mines and
plantations. Thomas sometimes referred to Malaya as 'the dollar
arsenal', pointing out that the USA
bought twenty-five times the quantity of goods that she sold to Malaya,
and in 1937 her purchases had totalled
no less than 235 million Straits dol-
lars. And, while his dispute with
General Bond was going on, he could
point out that during the quarter
ended 30th November alone, 137,331
tons of rubber were shipped to the
USA. It would be wrong to say that
Sir Shenton was completely unaware
of the danger of war. In his cables to
London he often expressed the view
that if only sufficient aircraft could
be sent these would provide the best
deterrent. The Air Officer Commanding Far East, Air-Marshal Babington,
was naturally in agreement with him.

Throughout 1940 there were conferences, meetings, appreciations and
a steady flow of paper but not a great
deal was done. And with the worsening situation in Europe, in Russia and
the Middle East, Far Eastern affairs
took last priority. However, in
October the Chiefs of Staff recommended a unified system of defence
for the Far East under a commander-

Major-General Gordon Bennett, commander Australian Forces

in-chief. The man selected for this vital post was Air-Marshal Sir Robert Brooke-Popham, formerly Governor of Kenya, who had been recalled to the service on the outbreak of war. The appointment did not fill many people with great enthusiasm. 'Brookham', as the Air-Marshal was known throughout the RAF, was a tall, gangling character with a red moustache and a shy, boyish manner, and he had come to this mammoth task too late. However, he had courage and was no fool and as soon as his headquarters were in operation he informed the Chiefs of Staff that Singapore could not be held for the Fleet unless the whole of Malaya were held also. To ensure security, the army would have to work closely with the RAF, and at the moment there was a grave shortage both of troops and aircraft. Against the Chiefs of Staff's own estimate of 336 aircraft, only forty-eight were available. To this the reply was that the figure would be achieved by the end of 1941, but Brooke-Popham remained sceptical and with good cause. One of the main obstacles to despatching reinforcements to the Far East at this time was Winston Churchill, who on 13th January 1941, wrote to the Chiefs of Staff: 'The political situation in the Far East does not seem to require, and the strength of the Air Force by no means permits, the maintenance of such large forces in the Far East at this time.' Brooke-Popham therefore never received the reinforcements he needed but at the same time it must be said that he seemed to respond to the 'never-never land' atmosphere of Singapore. His frequent optimistic statements, designed to deceive the Japanese, only added to the sense of unreality. The Japanese, of course, with their excellent Intelligence service, were never deceived for one moment.

However, reinforcements did come on an inadequate scale. In February Major-General Gordon Bennett brought the 8th Australian Division and more troopships were said to be on the way. Meanwhile Babington was replaced by Air Vice-Marshal Conway Pulford and Bond by Lieutenant-General A E Percival. One of the major figures in the drama to come, Percival was a colourless character, more a staff officer than a commander and certainly not a natural leader. He played everything by the rules, however ludicrous these might be, and if he did not lack urgency, he certainly lacked passion. He was not the man for a crisis and certainly not the man for a desperate campaign. How then, one might ask, had he achieved his high rank? To begin with he had shown great personal bravery in the First World War, winning the DSO and bar, the MC, and the French *Croix de Guerre*. Starting the war as a private soldier – he was twenty-seven years of age on enlistment – he had risen to command a battalion before it was over. His work during the troubles in Ireland in 1921 impressed both Churchill, then War Minister, and Lloyd George, the Prime Minister, and it was the latter who recommended him for a course at the Staff College, Camberley although he was over the normal age. Showing a remarkable aptitude for paper-work, he passed out well from the Staff College and went on to the Imperial Defence College. 1936 saw him in Malaya as Chief of Staff to General Dobbie, and here too his gift for turning out neatly phrased, crisp memoranda on any subject stood him in good stead. In fact, he was excellent in any job which did

Australian troops parade for lunch: their meat consumption rivalled that of the Americans

not involve contact with troops. Finishing his tour he returned to England but, with the outbreak of war, agitated for a more active appointment and someone in the War Office remembered that he had done well in Malaya. So the fateful decision was taken. He was appointed GOC in March 1941, and asked to fly out at three days' notice.

From the first he was dogged by ill luck. The flying boat detailed to take him broke down and it was five weeks before the necessary spares could be collected. On arrival at Singapore he found that very little had been done since he had left several years earlier. There was not a single aircraft available to help the army and the RAF requested him not to use any of their aircraft 'except on special occasions.' He found himself carrying out a tour of the peninsula in civilian airlines, or in small DH Moth aircraft, piloted by Volunteer Air Force men. It was now that he discovered that the northern airstrips had been sited in indefensible positions. Also that they were unused, as the RAF had not sufficient men or aircraft to occupy them. (Ample fuel supplies were laid on, however, which would in due course help the Japanese). Work on defence installations, both on the peninsula and on Singapore Island was almost at a standstill. The armed services were not permitted to pay coolies a high enough rate to attract them from the tin mines and rubber plantations. Altogether the result was that defence work, laid down as urgent by Dobbie in 1937, was still at the planning stage. And, of the fighter aircraft the government had

promised to send, there was no sign.

As it happened the despatch of Hurricanes was being discussed at this time in London by the Chiefs of Staff. The RAF representative argued that American Buffalo fighters would be a match for any Japanese aircraft likely to be encountered and this view was accepted. Being advised, Sir Robert Brooke-Popham remarked, 'We can get on alright with Buffaloes out here . . . Let England have the Super-Spitfires and Hyper-Hurricanes'. His Intelligence regarding Japanese aircraft was not only faulty, it was lacking altogether and the best one can say of him is that he was whistling to keep up his courage.

It was not only aircraft which were lacking in Malaya. When Percival had finished his initial tour he was to discover that there was not a single tank in the whole area.

But a facile optimism still pre-vailed in high quarters. On 9th September, Duff Cooper, a former diplomat and friend of Winston Churchill, arrived in Singapore with instructions 'to examine the existing arrangements for consultation and communication between the various British authorities in the area . . . and report how these could be made more effective'. On the 29th he held his first conference, and the brilliant array of military, naval, administrative and political talent accepted the view that Japan was concentrating her forces against Russia. She would be very unlikely, it was thought, to risk war with America, Britain and Holland simultaneously. Landings on the coast of Malaya seemed so unlikely as not to merit detailed discussion. This conference, of course, was held four years after General Dobbie's report had shown quite clearly that such landings were

quite feasible and nine months after Japanese preparations for the landings had begun on Hainan Island.

Despite the fall of the Konoye government on 16th October and its replacement by the extremist military administration of General Tojo, optimism still persisted. Even on 26th October, Churchill was telegraphing the Australian Prime Minister that Japan would not risk war until Russia was broken by the Germans. As an added deterrent, however, two of Britain's most powerful warships, HMSs *Prince of Wales* and *Repulse* would be moving to the Far East. What he did not mention was that the aircraft carrier HMS *Indomitable* designated to accompany them had been damaged at Kingston, Jamaica, and as no replacement was available the capital ships would be going alone.

The defence build-up on land was not impressive. To defend northern Malaya there was only 11th Indian Division (at present with only two brigades of partly trained troops, 6th and 15th Brigades), while on the east coast were 8th Brigade and 22nd Brigade of 9th Indian Division. With 28th Independent Infantry Brigade and some airfield defence troops, these weak formations formed General Heath's III Corps. They were fairly strong in artillery but had no tanks whatsoever – there was still not a single tank on the Malayan Peninsula or on Singapore Island. The Singapore Fortress troops consisted of Gordon Bennett's 8th Australian Division (two brigades only), 12th Independent Brigade and two Malay Infantry Brigades. Apart from a few British battalions like the Leicesters and the Argyll and Sutherland Highlanders, these troops were of mediocre or low quality, under-trained and indifferently led. The reinforcements still on their way were no better. And none had any idea of operating in jungle.

So the last days of peace slid by. Aided by General Heath, Percival tried to intensify training among his troops, tried unsuccessfully to prise money from the government to carry

Too few and too slow: Brewster Buffalos on Sembawang airfield, November 1941

43

Above: The arrival of Lady Diana and Duff Cooper.
Right: Indian troops practise creek crossing

out defence works, tried to construct large defensive positions at Jitra on the trunk road, forty miles south of the Siam border, and at Gurun twenty miles below it. But the businessmen still held sway in Malaya and did not want the troops near their plantations or their property. Any encroachment brought an immediate protest to the governor, Sir Shenton Thomas, which usually was upheld. Civilian life went on the same as ever. Anyone talking of war was accused of 'flapping'. For Brooke-Popham, for Percival and for Duff Cooper, and indeed for any service commander or even regimental officer to achieve anything in this atmosphere seemed almost impossible. It was like trying to swim through treacle.

Nothing illustrates their dilemna more than the muddle over 'Matador'. This was the plan to rush forward and seize Singora in Siam at the outbreak of hostilities, and hold it against any seaborne invasion. The troops detailed for this difficult task were Major-General Murray-Lyon's 11th Indian Division – who also had been detailed to hold the Jitra posi-

tion. How they could fulfil two completely conflicting roles was never settled. Nor was it settled exactly when the order to rush forward would be given. The government's policy was to refrain from any act of provocation, but the soldiers naturally wanted to reach Singora well before the Japanese to give themselves time to prepare their defence. The arguments went on until 5th December – the day after Yamashita and his army had sailed from Samah, and even then Brooke-Popham was told he must wait until the territory of Siam had been violated. The only concession was that he could order his troops forward without reference to London.

But this concession, like everything else, had come too late. Soon the bombs would be falling and the jungles would echo to the sound of machine guns and mortars. The Japanese menace, which, to borrow Winston Churchill's phrase had lain 'in a sinister twilight' was now launching its fury across the whole of the Western Pacific. The date was 8th December 1941.

Training: hard if not realistic. *Above left:* Indian gunners in a rubber plantation. *Above:* British troops on a coastal exercise. *Below:* Argyll and Sutherland Highlanders

The taste of reality

'The moon like a tray was sinking in the western sea and the deep red sun showed its face to the east. Samah harbour, shimmering with gold and silver waves, was as beautiful as a picture. The men on the convoy of twenty ships looked towards the bows . . . as the Navy formed in two lines to right and left of the convoy . . . This was surely the starting point which would determine the destiny of the nation for the next century. The die was cast.' So Colonel Tsuji described the scene as Yamashita's convoy set sail on the evening of 4th December. No doubt his sentiments reflected those held by many officers and men of Twenty-fifth Army.

During the night of the 4th/5th the voyage continued without incident. Soon after daylight came a signal from one of the escorting aircraft which read: 'No enemy sighted in south China sea', and this information was confirmed by several other reports. About 1000 hours, however, a message was given to Yamashita aboard the *Ryijo* which was not quite so comforting: 'Enemy submarine 196 miles off Saigon, speed 10 knots' – but later this proved to be a false alarm. The next incident did not occur until 1330 hours on the 6th, when a British aircraft flew alongside the convoy. This was a Hudson from Kota Bharu and though attacked by fighters it managed to escape. As Yamashita surmised, it signalled information concerning the size, course, and speed of the convoy, and some reaction could be expected. But now he was in luck, for the cloud cover increased and there were rainstorms which closed down visibility and made air reconnaissance impossible. At 1900 hours as planned the convoy swung north, as if heading into the Gulf of Siam, and when it changed course again next morning, the sky was still overcast and the weather had deteriorated. However, at 1010 hours Yamashita received a signal from Vice-Admiral Ozawa: 'Landing operations may go ahead as scheduled'.

The landing most affected by the

Singora: the Japanese assault troops seized fishing boats to get their men ashore

weather was at Kota Bharu, where Major-General Takumi would be in command. A signal relayed via the flagship indicated that although waves were now up to three feet high, conditions on the whole were good. In the early hours of the 8th, Yamashita learned that just before midnight the three transports carrying Takumi and his men had anchored off shore with their naval escort. What he was not told was that they were 2,000 yards to the south of their correct position and directly opposite the guns of 8th Indian Brigade. As Takumi recalled later: 'There was the dull light of an oval moon from over the sea to the east. A stiff breeze was blowing and I could hear it whistling in the radio aerials. The waves were now up to six feet'. Hoping that they would not increase any further, Takumi recalled that, according to the staff studies for the operation, waves of this dimension were the largest which could be accepted. Any more wind than was blowing at present and there would be chaos.

In fact, there was almost chaos as it was. The job of lowering the landing craft proved unexpectedly difficult, and once they had settled in the water they began swinging violently, shooting away from the ships' sides, then crashing back against them. The soldiers, scared of being crushed by the violent motion, shrieked and screamed in the darkness. To quote Takumi again: 'They were not only encumbered with life-jackets, but with rifles, light machine guns, ammunition and equipment. It was very hard to jump into the landing craft and even harder to move forward to our places. At intervals a soldier would fall screaming into the sea, and the sappers would fish him out'.

Not surprisingly in these circumstances it took an hour to launch the first wave of landing craft, which was under the command of Colonel Nasu. Patiently he waited on the choppy sea till the light signal came from Takumi that he could go ahead, acknowledged it, then shouted an order. Takumi continues: 'The landing craft pushed towards the coast in four lines. I could hear the sound of the engine above the waves. Then a red light signal flashed twice from among the palm trees on the coast. This was followed by rifle fire in seven or more places, then artillery and machine gun fire. The enemy seemed to be in strength'.

At 0200 hours, with the second wave still not launched the RAF came over and bombed the convoy. This so disturbed the Naval Escort Commander that he signalled Takumi demanding that the operation should be abandoned. Takumi refused, pointing out that he could not recall the troops already on shore and in any case the other waves would be away by 0600 hours. Until then the risks would have to be accepted. Reluctantly the Escort Commander gave way, but a few minutes later the *Awajisan Maru*, carrying Takumi and his headquarters, was hit by a bomb and began to heel over. Calling for a launch, Takumi was about to head for another transport ship but then changed his mind and headed straight for the shore. This was a courageous decision, but initially he had cause to regret it for his reception was a rough one. As he describes it: 'Many officers and men were killed or wounded, many jumped into the water before the craft had beached, and swam ashore. The enemy positions were about 100 yards from the water, and we could see that their posts were wired in. Their guns were pointing directly at us'. Other craft, as Takumi could see had beached just under the defence posts and in even more difficult water. Large numbers of men were going down in the heavy machine-gun fire. The sea was still so rough that the troops found it difficult to maintain their balance as they jumped from the craft and many were killed as they tried to scramble the few yards to dry land. 'There was the utmost confusion all along the beach', Takumi wrote 'but unit commanders realised that if they remained where they were, they would be killed to a man, so the order was "go on". The officers rushed inland and the men followed. Then the troops began to get round the back of the enemy positions and dig away the sand under the barbed wire. We also used grenades'.

It was almost 0400 hours before Yamashita received any news from

Takumi and this was a brief signal which read, 'Succeeded in landing at 0215 hours'. Yamashita was now aboard his ship in Singora harbour, having arrived at 0035 hours. There was no opposition and the troops disembarked in parade order. Yamashita went ashore himself at 0520 hours and his diary records:

'0800 hours. Entered the Governor's residence and ordered the police to be disarmed.

1300 hours. Succeeded in reaching a compromise agreement with the Thailand government.

2300 hours. Formalities completed allowing us to pass through Thailand'.

The Siamese government, of course, had no alternative but to meekly submit or see their country destroyed. What Yamashita describes as 'formalities' was simply a blunt demand.

While Yamashita was thus engaged, Twenty-fifth Army Staff were energetically getting ready for the advance south into Malaya. Colonel Tsuji (Operations Staff Officer) had filled trucks with troops disguised as civilian refugees and Siamese troops, and rushed them over the border to seize vital bridges before they could be blown up by the British.

By now Yamashita had heard that the air-strike against the American naval base at Pearl Harbor had been successful. He knew that naval supremacy in the Pacific had now passed to the Japanese, and in a matter of hours he would have air superiority over the whole of the Malayan peninsula and Singapore. Meanwhile Matsui and 5th Division, using the two trunk roads from Singora to Alor Star, and from Patani to Kroh, were streaming south, led by tank columns. Their objective was Jitra, in the province of Kedah, which lies near the western coast at the junction of the Kangar road with the main trunk road. Jitra, in fact, was the key to the whole campaign.

Now it is time to look at the first few hours of the war as they appeared from the British viewpoint. Seldom has there been a record more bedraggled by muddle, confusion and indecision. Reality broke through with painful slowness.

The Sunday morning edition of the *Malaya Tribune* carried a banner headline: 'Twenty-seven Japanese transports sighted off Cambodia point'. This was the southern tip of Indo-China and according to the Reuter message which was quoted below, the ships were steaming west, towards Siam or Malaya or both. To James Glover, the Yorkshireman who edited the paper, the news could only mean one thing: war. To Brooke-Popham, however, it meant no such thing, and soon he was on the phone to Glover protesting that, 'I consider it improper to print such alarmist views. The position isn't half so serious as the Tribune makes out'. Obviously this view was shared by the majority of the European community, for when Glover went along to the favourite Sunday morning rendezvous, the Sea View Hotel, there were the businessmen, the service officers, the civil servants and their ladies, relaxing over their stengahs, or gimlets, while the Chinese boys moved discreetly from table to table and the orchestra played a selection from Walt Disney's 'Snow White and the Seven Dwarfs'.

The military commanders were not at the hotel, but it cannot be said that they were reacting with great speed. On 6th December when the signal from the Hudson aircraft was received, Brooke-Popham did not launch Matador, but merely ordered a state of 'First Degree of Readiness'. So the troops of the 11th Indian Division stayed where they were in their camps on the Siamese frontier being drenched by the monsoon rains. Percival later wrote in his despatches that 'there was no undue cause for alarm, owing to the view that the Japanese expedition was directed against Siam'. On the evening of the 7th, another aircraft reported a Japanese cruiser sailing due west, and later, four destroyers and a merchant ship packed with troops on the deck going south. But still there was no alarm. And although the Japanese ambassador in Siam had already held an audience with the government, demanding a passage for Yamashita's troops through to Malaya, neither the British Legation nor even British Intelligence had got wind of this.

It was just after 0100 hours on

Singapore. *Above:* Japanese civilians leave for home, October 1941.
Right: Tamil workers try to clear the debris after an evening air raid

Monday the 8th that Sir Shenton Thomas heard that war had really come. From his headquarters in Fort Canning, General Percival was ringing up to give news that landings had commenced at Kota Bharu. According to one account, Thomas replied somewhat casually, 'Well, I suppose you'll shove the little men off', then phoned through instructions that all Japanese males were to be rounded up and security plans were to be put into operation. Three hours later there was another phone call, this time from Air Vice-Marshal Pulford, who gave the news that enemy aircraft were only twenty-five miles from Singapore. At 0415 hours the first bombs began to drop, and by the time the raid was over sixty-one people had been killed and 133 injured, most of them in the Chinese quarter.

The raid came as a shock, both to Thomas and the military commanders. Percival did not even know that there were enemy aircraft nearer

than French Indo-China, 600 miles away. So, the hours between the receipt of news from Kota Bharu and the commencement of the raid were wasted. No instructions were given to dim or switch off lights, and all the street lights in the city were full on. They were lit by gas and every single lamp had to be lit or put out by a man with a long pole – a process which took some hours. Later, in a prime example of administrative jabberwocky, Sir Shenton Thomas wrote, 'proclaiming of the first degree of readiness did not entail a blackout'. One wonders why he bothered to issue such instructions at all.

If there was civilian confusion in Singapore, there was military confusion farther north. Learning of the landing at Kota Bharu, Brooke-Popham had decided that it was quite useless to launch Matador, as 11th Division would find itself outflanked. So he cancelled the operation and ordered the troops back to Jitra to take up their defensive role. The

troops, it may be mentioned here, were exasperated and demoralised. They were inexperienced and lacked basic training, let alone specialised training in jungle warfare, and many units had lost their best NCOs and men, who had been sent back to India to help train new units. There was a long chain of command between Brooke-Popham and the troops on the border and at this moment it appeared somewhat tenuous. To begin with Brooke-Popham could not find Percival, the latter having chosen this moment to leave his headquarters to inform the Legislative Council of the situation. Once Percival had been found, he had to get back to his office and book a telephone call on the civilian line to the front. Orders did not reach Murray-Lyon, GOC 11th Division, until 1300 hours, which meant that ten precious hours had been lost. When the troops did eventually get back to Jitra, it was to find that the trenches there were water-logged and useless, so they had to start digging again. The lost ten hours gave victory at Jitra to the Japanese even before the shooting

had started. But, of course, the whole notion of Matador was ill-conceived. The troops on the frontier should have been withdrawn through positions already wired in and occupied by fresh units. The Official War History observes mildly that 'The need for a quick decision was not apparently realised at Headquarters, Malaya Command'. This, of course, is an understatement of staggering proportions. If a commander cannot give a quick decision when the enemy is at the gates, what can one say of him? No one had expected very much of Brooke-Popham, but Percival had given the first hint that despite his personal record in action and his success as a staff officer, he was no leader of men. From now on the hints were to come with increasing frequency.

Muddle in Singapore and muddle on the frontier. Already there had been muddle at Kota Bharu. The Indian troops of Brigadier Key's 8th Brigade had fought with great gallantry behind their heavily mined and wired defences, inflicting heavy casualties, but by 0400 hours the

Above left: Lieutenant-General Sir Lewis Heath, Commander III Indian
Corps. *Above right:* Lieutenant-General A E Percival, GOC Malaya.
Below: Admiral Tom Phillips with his Chief of Staff, Admiral Palliser, on left

Japanese had managed to secure two strong points. At dawn, when they were steadily expanding their hold, the brigade commander decided to launch a counter attack with the Dogra Frontier Force Rifles, who were to move eastwards along the beaches from Badang, while support was given by the guns sited near the airfield. The terrain, cut by rivers and swampy creeks, was difficult and the counterattack failed. Still the Dogras held on by the beach and although the situation there was confused, it was far from hopeless.

At frequent intervals during the day the airfield had been bombed and machine gunned. Then about 1600 hours rumours began to circulate that the Japanese had broken clean through the beach defences and were on the airfield perimeter. What may have happened is that a few stray bullets came over, and the troops – who had never been in action before – drew rash conclusions. More important, an officer who has yet to be identified, gave orders that the 'denial plan' was to be put into operation. So in a matter of minutes the buildings were set on fire and the ground staff piled into their vehicles and drove away. Learning of this, the wing commander and Brigadier Key carried out a rapid reconnaissance to find that there were no Japanese near the airfield. But it was too late; the men could not be recalled. Even worse, the stocks of bombs and petrol had still to be destroyed, and the runways put out of action. The aircraft had already been withdrawn to Kuantan, on orders from Air Headquarters, so now the Indian troops resolutely holding out on the beaches were denied all air cover.

The next move was inevitable. When more Japanese troopships arrived off the coast, Brigadier Key decided to withdraw. The Japanese had achieved their beach-head in just under twenty-four hours. Fortunately, the 73rd Field Battery had gone to the airfield and set fire to the petrol stores by shelling at point-blank range but the runways were still usable.

After darkness the artillery, together with the anti-aircraft guns, got away without trouble. But the three forward battalions had a rough time, floundering in the creeks and swamps in heavy rain. Taking up a defensive line a few miles inland, they were heavily mortared and then attacked by infantry and to avoid the danger of encirclement were forced to retreat again. The airfields at Gong Kedah and Machang were abandoned. By 11th December, Key had concentrated his brigade astride the railway running south of Machang and here he took up a strong defensive position. However, Key's divisional commander, Major-General A E Barstow, had already asked his superior, General Heath, for permission to withdraw to Lipis in central Malaya. The brigade's primary task, he pointed out, had been to defend the northern airfields, and now that these had been abandoned it should shorten its tenuous line of communications. Heath in turn sought permission from Percival, but again the latter was not there when he was wanted. He had left his headquarters and taken the train back to Singapore. In the words of the Official Historians 'his absence from the front at this critical juncture was inopportune'. It was worse than inopportune; it was bad generalship.

The war in the air had gone even worse than the war on the ground. A bomber force sent to bomb Singora had achieved little success and lost heavily to the fighters. The RAF had not been able to provide effective cover for the northern airfields and the warning system proved utterly inadequate. Time and again aircraft were caught on the ground and during 8th December alone the operational strength of aircraft operating from the northern airfields was reduced from 110 to fifty. From airfields around Singora and the northern airfields as they came into operation again, the Japanese rapidly built up their strike force. Soon the sky would be theirs.

In this atmosphere of confusion and disintegration, it is not surprising that rumours and false reports went on multiplying; and the most serious of these was of a landing at Kuantan on the east coast, 200 miles north of Singapore. Events marched as follows.

Lockheed Hudsons of the Royal
Australian Air Force on a training flight

Soon after mid-day on the 8th, Admiral Tom Phillips, commander of Z Force, consisting of HMSs *Prince of Wales, Repulse* and four destroyers, called a conference aboard his flag ship. Information had just been received of the landings at Singora and Kota Bharu, and Phillips gave the opinion that, granted fighter cover, the Royal Navy could smash the Japanese transports and their escorts. In any case, Z Force could not remain inactive at such a juncture. So at 1735 hours the grey ships left Singapore harbour and steamed north-west. Just before leaving, the Admiral was warned that the RAF was doubtful if fighter cover could be provided off Singora and the following day he learned that the north Malaya airfields had been lost. Courageously Phillips decided that if his force were not sighted by aircraft on the 9th he would attempt to carry out his mission, and at 1600 hours ordered course to be set due north. At this time the weather was overcast and there were heavy rainstorms, but a few hours later the sky cleared and then three aircraft came into view. All hope of surprise was lost and, denied air cover, the ships would come under heavy attack from the Japanese squadrons long before they reached their targets. So at 2015 hours Phillips decided that the risks were too great and reluctantly turned back for Singapore. Now signals giving news of the 'landing' at Kuantan arrived, and the admiral decided that he must take action. Having seen him steaming north before nightfall, it was hardly likely, he reasoned, that the Japanese would suspect him so far south as Kuantan and there was a good chance of achieving surprise. So just before 0100 hours on the 10th he altered course again – for Kuantan.

But the admiral had underrated both Japanese efficiency and their determination that the *Prince of Wales* and the *Repulse* should not upset their plans. Submarines had sighted Z Force early on the 9th and given details of course and speed.

Below: HMS *Prince of Wales.* **Above:** HMS *Repulse.* Fine ships, but the aircraft-carrier was still in Jamaica leaving them unprotected

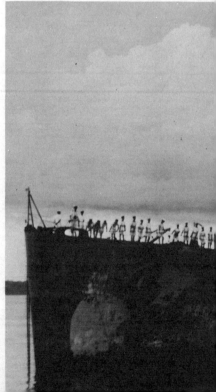

Admiral Kondo had at once ordered 7th Cruiser Squadron to steam south-west to intercept Phillips. Aircraft of 22nd Air Flotilla armed with torpedoes took off for a night attack, but, however, they failed to find Z Force because of the change of course, and returned to Saigon. But then at 0210 hours on the 10th another submarine sighted the British ships and fired five torpedoes, all of them missing. To his fury Admiral Kondo realised that his ships would never catch Phillips and so ordered 22nd Air Flotilla to attack at dawn. Immediately on receipt of the signal the flotilla commander sent out twelve reconnaissance aircraft and just before 1030 hours one of these found Phillips. Keeping the ships in sight, the pilot signalled his headquarters, and before dawn the strike-force rose into the air: thirty-four high-level bombers and fifty-one torpedo-bombers. Confidently they headed south-west across the sea.

Meanwhile Phillips and Z Force had been steaming towards Kuantan, which they reached at 0800 hours. No sign of an invasion fleet could be found, so Phillips decided to carry out a sweep to the north and east to examine some barges which had earlier been spotted in the distance. At 1000 hours reports of hostile aircraft were received, and twenty minutes later the radar operator aboard the *Repulse* reported dots on his screen. Aircraft were approaching from the south-west. By 1100 hours nine could be seen in the sky, and systematically they began a high-level bombing attack on the *Repulse*. The accuracy was good and bombs fell close on either side and one right on to the deck, though fortunately it failed to pierce the armour plating. Just before mid-day a squadron of torpedo-bombers came in and the great capital ships began manoeuvring to 'comb the tracks'. The *Repulse* was successful, but as the *Prince of Wales* veered to port, there were two enormous explosions. Her propeller

Below: Vice-Admiral Nobuyuki Kendo, (right) Commander Southern Force on his way to an audience with the Emperor. **Right:** The end of the *Repulse*

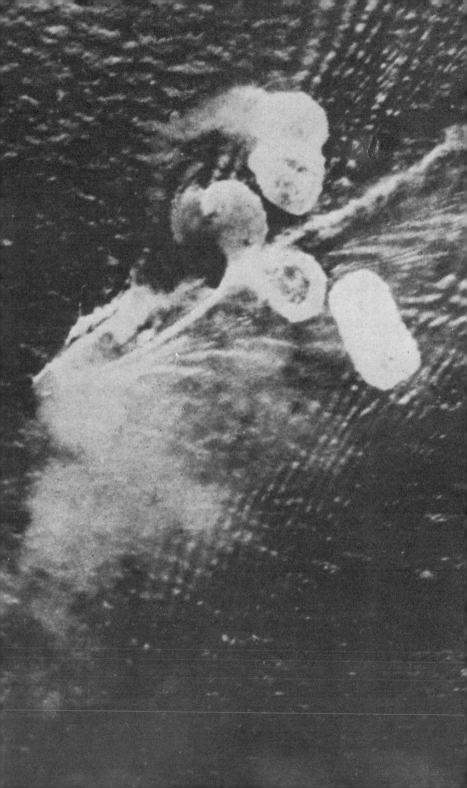

shafts immediately stopped turning and she went out of control. A few minutes later she was listing to port and her speed went down to fifteen knots. At 1210 hours her captain signalled 'Not under control'. Meanwhile the *Repulse* had come under heavy attack from both bombers and torpedo-bombers, but showing incredible skill of manoeuvre, her skipper, Captain Tennant, had managed to escape damage from both. More and more aircraft came. The *Prince of Wales* was hit by three more torpedoes and then it was the turn of the *Repulse*. Aircraft were coming at her from all directions, wave after wave, and it was only a matter of time before a torpedo caught her. Losing power of manoeuvre, she was hit again and again. The rudder was jammed, and Captain Tennant, realising that the situation was hopeless, ordered his crew to go on deck and the floats to be cast loose. What happened next is best told in his own words:

'Men were now pouring up on deck. They had all been warned twenty-four hours before to carry or wear their life-saving apparatus. When the ship had a thirty-degree list to port I looked over the starboard side of the bridge and saw the commander and two or three hundred men collecting on the starboard side. I never saw any sign of panic or ill discipline. I told them from the bridge how well they had fought the ship and wished them good luck. The ship hung on for at least a minute and a half or two minutes with a list of about 60 or 70 degrees to port and then rolled over at 1233 pm.'

Out of sixty-nine officers and 1,240 men, forty-two and 754 respectively were picked up by the destroyers. Many had been killed already and the rest were drowned.

Meanwhile with its decks awash, the stricken *Prince of Wales* had been steaming north, attacked again and again by the bombers. By 1300 hours she began to settle and her captain gave the order to abandon ship. All except twenty officers and some 300 men were rescued, but there was no sign of Admiral Tom Phillips and Captain Leach. Perhaps they did not wish to be saved. When the squadron of Buffaloes, detailed to give air cover,

arrived from Singapore, the sea was littered with wreckage and men floating around in the water waiting to be picked up by the destroyers. Curiously enough, the men were far from dispirited, as the pilot reported later:

'It was obvious that the three destroyers were going to take hours to pick up those hundreds of men clinging to bits of wreckage and swimming around in filthy, oily water. About all this the threat of another bombing and machine gun attack was imminent. Every one of those men must have realised that. Yet as I flew round every man waved and put up his thumb as I flew over him . . . It shook me, for here was something above human nature.'

The loss of Z force was one of the greatest disasters suffered in the whole history of the Royal Navy. For the British in Malaya, the loss of their two great ships meant the end of a legend, for they had been told that the arrival of the fleet would ensure their security and now it had been wiped out in a matter of hours, just as the American fleet had been wiped out at Pearl Harbor. When Duff Cooper broadcast from Singapore that night that the grievous loss should make everyone fight harder, there was hollow laughter among the troops and their moral sank even lower. What on earth had their leaders been doing? And the admirals too? And where were all the aircraft? No one could give them any satisfactory answer or even a ray of hope. All they could do was trudge on and fight in the drenching rain.

To Winston Churchill the disaster was without parallel and later he wrote:

'In all the war I never received a more direct shock . . . As I turned over and twisted in bed the full horror of the news sank in upon me. There were no British or American capital ships in the Indian Ocean or the Pacific except the American survivors of Pearl Harbor, who were hastening back to California. Over all this vast expanse of waters Japan was supreme, and we everywhere were weak and naked.'

HMS *Prince of Wales:* **hit by three torpedoes she keels over**

Captain (later Vice-Admiral)
W G Tennant, captain of the *Repulse*.
Right: Crew leave the *Repulse*.
The Japanese now ruled the
eastern Pacific

Like every other naval disaster, the loss of Z force has its mysteries. Why did not Tom Phillips signal Singapore when he knew that he was being shadowed at 1020 hours on the 10th? Why did he not signal his intention to head for Kuantan? And, once enemy aircraft were sighted on the radar screen, why did he not call up the Buffaloes of 453 Squadron, which were waiting at Sembawang, to give him air cover? The information that the battleships were under attack came from Captain Tennant and that was too late . . . far too late.

The news that the *Prince of Wales* and the *Repulse* had been sunk for the trifling loss of three aircraft was received in Japan with enormous enthusiasm. It was a unique victory quite unprecedented in all military history. To Yamashita, whose head-quarters still lay at Singora, it meant that his line of communications, running back to Samah, was secure. Meanwhile, his troops were racing south towards Jitra and he was confident that if victory were achieved here, nothing would hold them before Singapore.

Disaster at Jitra

On the outbreak of war the politician and ex-diplomat Duff Cooper had been appointed by Churchill to the post of Resident Minister for Far Eastern Affairs and was given cabinet rank. His main job was to preside over a War Council, but he was also to relieve the service commanders of their 'extraneous responsibilities', give political guidance, and settle any matters on the spot which could not be referred to Whitehall because of the time factor. His duties, however, so the brief warned, would not cut across the responsibilities of service heads or 'of His Majesty's representatives in the Far East'. The brief was not an easy one, but Duff Cooper, who was very intelligent and had an aggressive streak in him, decided that the only possible job for a War Council was to run the war and, at the first meeting on 10th December made no bones about this. Immediately there was opposition from Sir Shenton Thomas who denied that the Council had executive powers. Brooke-Popham sided with him, telling Duff Cooper that he would continue to take his orders from Whitehall and not from any civilian. So the President of the War Council and his two principal colleagues became sworn enemies, with the result that the three services did not work together now, any more than in the past. It almost seemed as if some of the senior commanders preferred defeat to co-operation with their colleagues. In any case, the War Council proved a failure.

To return to 11th Division which had taken up its position astride the road junction at Jitra. Though the best position in the area, this was far from ideal, and had been chosen because it covered the airfield at Alor Star and a group of smaller fields further south. Alor Star was one of the most famous airfields in the Far East at this time, since it had been used in dozens of record breaking flights and air races. Amy Johnson had staged here during her flight from England to Australia in 1930, as had Kingsford-Smith, Bert Hinkler, Ray Parer and others. It was also used on the famous England-Australia Air Race of 1934, and the Dutchmen Moll and Parmentier landed here, the Americans, Roscoe Turner and Clyde Pangborn, and the winning Englishmen, Scott and Black. Alor Star, with its installations and reserve of fuel and supplies, was of immense importance to the RAF.

As already recorded, 11th Division came back from Matador to find the trenches water-logged, and no barbed wire or other defensive measures taken care of. The anti-tank mines were still waiting in piles and not a yard of telephone cable had been run out. Hurriedly they set to work, squelching over the soggy ground, and with the heavy rain pouring down their necks. Every moment counted, and as they realised only too well, there were not many to go.

Murray-Lyon had deployed his division with 15th Brigade on the right, 6th Brigade on the left and 28th Brigade in reserve. The frontage ran from the jungle-covered hills through the open paddy fields to the sea, a total distance of 24,000 yards of which 6th Brigade covered three-quarters. Supporting the infantry were two batteries of 155th Field Regiment and a battery of 22nd Mountain Regiment. There was also 80th Anti-Tank Regiment, less one of its batteries. Detachments of 1/14th Punjab were covering the main position, and from 0800 hours on the 11th these came under attack from the Japanese. Soon their leading sections had been overrun and two anti-tank guns were lost. Brigadier Garrett (15th Brigade) decided to withdraw the unit through the main position. At 1500 hours, however, Murray-Lyon ordered him to take up a position near Nangka, two miles before Jitra, and the Punjabis began trudging back in the rain. Then at 0430 hours the Japanese struck with a column of infantry led by tanks, which burst down the road at speed. Soon it had mown down the rear-guard and caught up with the main column which immediately broke formation and panicked. Most of the Punjabis had never seen a tank in their lives and their only instinct was to run for cover. Worse still, a section of 2nd Anti-Tank Battery was caught with its guns limbered up – or certainly

Brooke-Popham and Duff Cooper:
the commander resented the civilian

Above: An Indian battalion on the march. The best men were back in India. *Below:* Still time for ceremony on Singapore: Australian troops are inspected

before it had managed to get off a round. The Japanese rushed on until their leading tank was knocked out by anti-tank rifles, and they came up against the 2/1st Gurkhas holding the main outpost position at Asun.

Now a stiff fight developed, but the Japanese retained the initiative. Attacking the Gurkhas both frontally and from the flanks, they soon succeeded in clearing the road and went on savagely attacking position after position. The Gurkha battalion fragmented and all attempts at an orderly withdrawal failed. Like the Punjabis before them, the men had to make a detour through the jungle in small groups and rejoined their brigade next morning.

Meanwhile there had been another disastrous muddle. After dark on the 11th the outpost troops of 6th Brigade were withdrawing to the main Jitra position under orders, taking with them their transport, seven anti-tank guns and four mountain guns. Their route ran across a stream at Manggoi, to the west of Jitra, and here the bridge had been prepared for demolition. Hearing the column approach, the jittery officer in charge imagined it must be the Japanese and promptly blew the bridge. As there were no materials to repair it, the transport and guns had to be abandoned. Seldom in the history of war can there have been such an unbroken skein of muddle, confusion and stupidity. And it was by no means fully unravelled.

It is interesting to compare British accounts of the debacle with those of the Japanese. According to Tsuji, who was on the spot, the unit which ploughed through the Punjabis near Nangka was Lieutenant–Colonel Saeki's Reconnaissance Battalion, supported by ten medium tanks. Of the incident involving 2nd Anti-Tank Battery, he says:

'Ten guns with their muzzles turned towards us were lined up on the road, but beside them we could not find one man of their crews. The enemy appeared to be sheltering from the heavy rain under the rubber trees . . . and through this slight negligence they suffered a crushing defeat.'

Whether the guns were limbered up, or whether it was as Tsuji says, the disgrace was the same and the loss just as grievous. With two battalions cut up before the main battle had begun, Murray-Lyon was robbed of his divisional reserve.

As soon as it was dark, Saeki sent out a patrol under Lieutenant Otto to reconnoitre the position held by 2/9th Jats on the British right flank. An hour later Otto returned with the news that the companies were wired in strongly, but there were gaps between the forward positions. From what he had heard in the darkness, he added, the enemy troops were still settling in and he thought that a night attack would have a good change of succeeding. Saeki accepted this advice and put in an attack two hours after dark, but the volume of machine gun and artillery fire caught the infantry by surprise and they came to a halt. When the reserve companies were thrown in, they made no impression either and Saeki, now somewhat shaken, talked of committing suicide by leading a forlorn rush against the enemy. Though a senior officer dissuaded him, the surviving men of the Reconnaissance Battalion sensed the lack of decision and were momentarily shaken. However, when Saeki called for an attack in the centre by the whole unit, supported by mortars, the men responded, and after some heavy fighting succeeded in driving a deep wedge into the British positions. However, the Leicesters and the 2/2nd Gurkhas held on and again the attack ground to a halt. Then the Carrier Platoon of the 2nd East Surreys counterattacked, checking an attempt to envelope the Leicesters.

'In this hour of trial the General Officer Commanding calls upon all ranks of Malaya Command for a determined and sustained effort to safeguard Malaya and the adjoining British territories. The eyes of the Empire are upon us. Our whole position in the Far East is at stake. The struggle may be long and grim, but let us resolve to stand fast, come what may, and prove ourselves worthy of the great trust which has been placed in us.'

By the 12th Percival's Order of the Day, issued forty-eight hours previously, had reached the troops at Jitra. It made no impact whatsoever. The battle had begun in muddle and was continuing in confusion. Percival was little more than a name. Wet and hungry, and peering through the jungle towards the Japanese, the troops, whether British or Indian, had little faith in their leaders or hope in the eventual outcome of the campaign.

The instinct of fighting troops is usually sound in these matters, and even as they were reading the Order of the Day, their Divisional Commander, Murray-Lyon, was pressing General Heath, GOC III Corps, for permission to withdraw to Gurun, thirty miles to the south. His reason was, he said, that it had been impressed upon him that his division was the only formation available to defend northern Malaya and he must not take risks. The troops he added,

Japanese Medium Type 94 Tank
First introduced in 1934, this tank was used extensively in China and continued to be used in Burma and Malaya as late as 1942. *Weight:* 15 tons. *Crew:* Five men. *Armour:* 17mm maximum. *Armament:* One 57mm gun, one 7.7mm machine gun in the rear of the turret and one 7.7mm machine gun in the hull. *Ammunition:* 100 rounds of 57mm and 2,750 rounds of 7.7mm. *Speed:* 28 mph. *Engine:* 160 hp Mitsubishi air-cooled diesel. *Range of action:* 100 miles

were dispirited at having to fight superior forces supported by tanks. He was also worried about his communications – that is, that the Japanese would get round behind him and cut the road. Heath at this time was still in Singapore with Percival and put the matter to him. Percival was against such a long retreat, convinced that it would have a bad effect both on the troops themselves and the civilian population, and he was supported by the War Council.

But though he managed to impress his will on this occasion, Percival did not dominate as an army commander should and displayed an increasing tendency to knuckle under to Heath. Gordon Bennett, the Australian commander, has written:

'Heath ... had a stronger personality than Percival and generally managed to impose his will on that of Percival. Throughout the conferences which I attended [Heath] urged retirements. In fact, one of his brigadiers had been detailed to reconnoitre successive lines of retreat down the peninsula ... [On one occasion] I suggested the only way to deal with the situation was to attack. He ridiculed the idea.'

Allowing for the possibility that Bennett (whose troops had not yet come into action while Jitra was being fought) was trying to justify his own conduct, there still must be some truth in his statement.

Apart from failing to impress his will, Percival failed, while the action at Jitra was in progress, to exercise any tactical imagination. By 12th December at least, it must have been obvious that 11th Division was taking such a hammering that retreat was only a matter of time. Why did he not select the strongest possible defensive position on the road back to Singapore, use every available man to fortify it and stock it up for a long siege. Why did he not construct a series of jungle bases from which the Japanese could be attacked from the flank and rear as

Japanese Light Type 95 Tank
This tank continued in service in Malaya and in the Pacific until 1943. As with other Japanese light tank designs, the Type 95 was very cramped and lightly armoured. *Weight:* 10 tons. *Crew:* Three men. *Armour:* 14mm maximum. *Armament:* One 37mm gun, one 7.7mm machine gun in the rear of the turret and one 7.7mm machine gun in the hull. *Ammunition:* 130 rounds of 37mm and 2,970 rounds of 7.7mm ammunition. *Speed:* 28 mph. *Engine:* 110 hp Mitsubishi diesel. *Range of action:* 100 miles

they carried out their hooks? Why did he not consider guerilla warfare in such ideal country for it. Colonel Spencer Chapman, later famous for his guerilla exploits, had already put up constructive suggestions, only to be told that Malaya Command had no interest whatsoever in such notions. So the pattern would go on repeating itself; fight, retreat, fight again, retreat . . . until there was nowhere else to retreat to.

By noon on the 12th, Major-General Kawamura, commander 9th Infantry Brigade had arrived on the scene and ordered 41st Regiment to attack down the eastern side of the road, while 40th Regiment attacked on the other side. The operation would take place after dark. Meanwhile, Saeki had been in action again and by 1500 hours was threatening the flanks of the Jats and the Leicesters. The latter unit, however, had fought well and was full of confidence. When, at about 1515 hours, they received orders to retire behind a stream called the Sungei Jitra, they protested violently. However, Murray-Lyon was insistent, and so they came back, and the Jats too. This was yet another great blow to morale.

But the damage did not end there. Going back down the road to his headquarters that evening, Murray-Lyon found the transport column panicking because of rumours that the Japanese tanks had broken through again. Later on rumours reached him that the Jats and Punjabis had been overrun and although these were quite untrue, they still made their impact. Fearing that the road would soon be cut behind his division, Murray-Lyon decided that he must get it behind a viable tank obstacle by the following day. So at 1930 hours he signalled Heath, asking permission to withdraw behind the Sungei Kedah at Gurun. Heath, still in Singapore with Percival, supported the application and Percival gave way. The following signal was sent:

'It is decided that your task is to fight for the security of north Kedah. It is estimated that you are opposed

Japanese infantry attack Alor Star: with Jitra lost there was nothing to stop them

73

by only one Japanese division. Consider the best solution may be to hold up the advance of enemy tanks on good obstacles and dispose your forces to obtain considerable depth on both roads and to obtain scope for your superior artillery. Reserves for employment in the divisional area are being expedited.'

With this signal – the naivety of which is scarcely credible – was sent permission for Murray-Lyon to withdraw at his discretion. So at 2200 hours he sent orders for his men to go back to behind the Sungei Kedahl at Alor Star, some fifteen miles back.

Again the weary troops collected their ammunition and their kit and streamed down the road in drenching rain. They were tired and bewildered. The Leicesters were furious at being brought back from their position. Units became scattered and fragmented in the darkness, and all order and cohesion was lost. Some unit commanders, fearing congestion on the road, took their units via the

Japanese 2.2mm machine gun, gas operated and air cooled

railway track to the west; some went down to the beach and tried to get south in small craft; and some did not even get the order to retreat. It was next morning before these realised what had happened, and then they had to break with the enemy in a hurry, leaving behind a good deal of their ammunition and equipment. Though a Japanese attempt to interfere with the withdrawal was dealt with decisively by the 2/2nd Gurkha Rifles, the retreat was a mistake and a disaster. 11th Indian Division would never be the same again.

As for the action at Jitra itself, this had proved possibly the biggest disgrace to British/Indian armies since Chillianwala in the Second Sikh War of 1848. Hundreds of men had been lost, as well as guns, equipment and transport. But the most galling thing was that Matsui had not even been forced to deploy the entire 5th Division: the job had been done by the advance guard whose strength totalled no more than two battalions, and a company of tanks. Their total losses were under fifty. Mastui wrote in his diary: 'The enemy troops have

no fighting spirit . . . they are glad to surrender . . . they are relieved to be out of the war.' As for Yamashita, he had written in his diary on 10th November 'If Indian troops are included in the British forces defending Malaya, the job should be easy.' Now he considered his prophecy justified.

The main reasons for the defeat have already been indicated; the wide dispersal of the unit positions, which allowed the Japanese to effect deep penetrations; the scramble after operation Matador was abandoned; and the short time allowed 11th Division to occupy and prepare its position. Undoubtedly Murray-Lyon made a disastrous mistake in committing two battalions to outpost duties without the cover of an anti-tank obstacle. When these were cut up, he lost his divisional reserve and so had no troops left with which to counter the enemy penetration. Apart from this the troops were badly trained and reacted to any rumour which swept through their ranks; and their officers lacked the ability to handle them in the field. Communica-tions between battalions and divisional headquarters seem to have been primitive and, in the absence of radio sets, runners , who frequently got lost, had to be relied on.

It might be mentioned here that neither side was well equipped with maps. The British maps were large-scale, but mostly dated from about 1915 and did not show the recent development of estates. The Japanese relied on small-scale maps mostly copied from school atlases, but their officers were used to these – the Japanese army had always fought with inadequate maps. Once contact was made, however, the Japanese worked excellently from the ground and were fortunate in capturing a British map with all the defensive positions marked. After their training on Hainan island, thick country did not worry them, though they had no more love of jungle than any other troops.

Most important was the fact that they believed in their commanders and they held the initiative. In the battles to come they had no intention of letting it slip.

The long retreat

The Allied situation in northern Malaya, as a watery sun came up on the morning of 13th December, was not a happy one. Covered by rearguards found by 28th Brigade, the rest of 11th Indian Division was streaming back to man a position behind the Sungei Kedah at Alor Star. Many of the troops had lost or thrown away their arms and were numbly drifting around trying to find their units. Meanwhile, Japanese snipers, dressed as Malays, had got into the jungle flanking the position, and it was some time before these could be winkled out.

Obviously, to halt, let alone slow up the Japanese advance, it was vital to blow the road and rail bridges over the Sungei Kedah and during the night of the 12th/13th charges had been put into position. Soon after dawn, Murray-Lyon and his Sapper officer waited by the road bridge as the last troops streamed over, and was surprised when two Japanese motorcyclist roared down the road towards them. These were soon despatched, and Murray-Lyon ordered the bridges to be blown. The road bridge went up without trouble but the railway bridge, though damaged, managed to remain upright. At this moment an armoured train came down the line from the north, and so it was hoped it would complete the destruction. But to everyone's amazement, it jumped the gap in the rails and went on out of sight. So more explosives had to be laid before the bridge went down.

It was only just in time, for at this moment the Japanese advance guard appeared and the leading troops tried hard to cross the river. A few succeeded but were driven back by a counterattack launched by the 2/9th Gurkha Rifles. Still, looking at his tired, soaked and disorganised troops, Murray-Lyon decided that they were in no shape to withstand a prolonged defence, and the only hope was to break contact with the enemy and go back twenty miles to Gurun. Here perhaps, there would be time to reorganise. Percival might carry out his pledge to send up reinforcements from Singapore.

So that night the division went back again with the rain still bucket-

ting down, and the transport jammed on the single road. Though the position at Gurun had been reconnoitred, no defence works had been dug and the exhausted troops would have to start all over again. The exact position chosen lay astride the main road and railway, about three miles to the north of Gurun, and ran from the jungle-clad slopes of Kedah

Peak on the left to the jungle some two miles away on the right. Though not a position of great natural strength, it could have been worse. But what 11th Division needed more than anything was time . . . time to dig . . . time to put out wire and mines . . . time to clear a field of fire . . . and more than anything time to sleep.

Unhappily for them it was to be

Japanese infantry: if the bridge is not finished, human columns will serve

denied. Yamashita's engineering regiments, after their thorough training on Hainan, were working with tremendous speed repairing the Allied demolitions. So it was that soon after lunch on the 14th, when the last of the stragglers had barely fetched up, a dozen truck loads of Japanese infantry, supported by three tanks, came lumbering down the road. Murray-Lyon had expected the Japanese to take three days at least to repair the road bridge over the Sungei Kedah – and now here they were, barely thirty hours later. 6th Brigade were holding the road and railway line (with 28th Brigade on their right and 15th Brigade, which was now down to 600 men, in reserve). It was the anti-tank gunners, however, who opened fire first, knocking out the leading tank. The other two retired, but the infantry, who had now deployed, launched a furious attack on the Punjabis to the left of the road. Two hours later, after being heavily

reinforced, they managed to penetrate the Indians' positions, and individual soldiers could soon be seen running back. The battalion's morale was pretty low, and the accuracy of the Japanese mortars worried the Indian jawans. Also they were desperately tired. But now the brigade commander, Brigadier Lay, recognised that unless something were done soon, the position would fragment, so with great courage he organised a counter-attack and led it himself. The position around Milestone 20 was stabilised, and the sight of the Brigadier in action did a good deal to restore confidence.

Meanwhile the Corps commander, General Heath, had come forward at last to meet Murray-Lyon at his headquarters a few miles to the south of Gurun. Here the latter argued that his troops were quite un-

Some Malayans collaborated with the enemy: Indians guard suspects awaiting interrogation

fit to carry out a series of battles interspersed with long retreats. What must be done, he urged, was to make a long retreat by lorry to a selected concentration area. Once the formation had been rested and reorganised, it could fight again – but not before then. In principle Heath agreed, but laid down that the immediate task of 11th Division was to hold the Japanese at Gurun. There was no need to worry about the line of communications he added; 12th Brigade had now come under his command and would be used to block the roads from Kroh and Grik to the east. That night Heath telephoned Percival, recommending that 11th Division should go back sixty miles or more to behind the Perak River. A temporary stand could be made on the Muda River to give time for the garrison to be evacuated from Penang Island. Meanwhile, the Japanese would be held up by a long series of demolitions along the road and railway. To this, Percival agreed that a further retirement might be inevitable but told Heath that 11th Division must not go back behind the Muda River without his permission.

Again the Japanese did not wait on events. Soon after midnight they launched a sustained mortar bombardment, then attacked straight down the road, through the Punjabi positions. Before long they had broken through and penetrated positions held by the 2nd East Surreys to the south. Here they reached the regimental headquarters, killing the commanding officer and his staff and went on to deal with 6th Brigade headquarters. With the exception of Brigadier Lay, who was out with a unit, everyone was wiped out. Next morning, with a gaping hole in the centre of the position, Brigadier Carpendale of 28th Brigade got together all the troops he could find and managed to hold the enemy. But when Murray-Lyon arrived, he at once ordered a further withdrawal to a position seven miles back, which was covered by a mixed force of infantry and cavalry. Before long, however, he realised that 28th Brigade was now the only formation under his command in a fit state to obey orders, and he decided to withdraw behind the Muda River that night. Fortunately

the Japanese, who had suffered heavily from artillery fire during the day, did not follow up. By the morning of the 16th the remnants of 11th Division were back in their new positions. Needless to add they had lost more men and equipment by the confusion of yet another retreat and by premature demolitions.

This decision meant that the island of Penang, already under heavy bombardment from the air, would have to be evacuated. The blow to civilian morale was a serious one, but there was no alternative. Already, following the destruction of power stations and the contamination of water supplies, there was the fear of cholera and typhoid. There was no need for the evacuation to be carried out in such disorder and with such carelessness. When the Japanese arrived they found dozens of powered craft, junks, and barges, which they soon put to good use for the seaborne operations.

On 18th December, by which time 11th Division had retreated yet another thirty miles to a position behind the Krian River, Percival was forced to carry out a major review of his strategy. It was now clear to him that apart from Matsui's 5th Division on the trunk road, he was facing another division on the Patani-Kroh-Grik Road – running into the trunk road from the east at Kuala Kangsar – and a third on the east coast in Kelentan. To meet this powerful striking force he had the remains of 11th Division, now exhausted, two brigades on the east coast, Gordon Bennett's 8th Australian Division (two brigades only) in Johore at the southern end of the peninsula, and the garrison troops on Singapore Island. Now it must be remembered that Percival's primary task was not the defence of Malaya, but the Naval base on Singapore Island. But how, in the present circumstances, was this to be achieved? If he used the Australians to relieve 11th Division, then Johore would be denuded, but if he did not there was the chance that the Japanese would burst through before reinforcements could arrive. Here was another problem. The further the Japanese came south, the more airfields would fall into their hands, and from these they could threaten the convoys bringing in the reinforcements. So, having to make the best of a bad job, Percival was forced to ask 11th Division to try and hold the Japanese as far north as possible until the reinforcements arrived.

But when would these come? The most optimistic forecast was mid-January, and after arrival the men would need time to unload their kit, get organised and accustom themselves to the hot sticky climate. And this in turn meant that the exhausted, demoralised troops on the northern front would have to keep fighting for yet another month, denied air cover or the support of a single tank and increasingly out-numbered.

How could they possibly be made to keep going? The best chance Percival decided was to bring them back to behind a viable tank obstacle – the Perak River, which runs down to the sea through Kuala Kangsar. Here 12th Indian Brigade would join the division, and the depleted 6th Brigade would be merged into 15th Brigade. But reorganisations, necessary as they were, did not give the troops any rest and their condition continued to deteriorate. During the retreat to the Perak River an officer wrote:

'It can't go on like this. The troops are absolutely dead-beat. The only rest they are getting is that of an uneasy coma as they squat in crowded lorries which jerk their way through the night. When they arrive they tumble out and have to get straight down to work. They are stupid with sleep, and have to be smacked before they can connect with the simplest order. Then they move like automatons or cower down as a Jap aeroplane flies two hundred feet above them.'

The behaviour of the troops, indeed the whole situation was not lost on the Asiatic population. The British hold on their country, which had seemed so strong and permanent, was now collapsing and European superiority revealed as a myth.

Yamashita was not greatly concerned by the obstacle presented by the Perak River for he knew that his enemy was too weak to cover it on a broad front. So he ordered 4th Guards Regiment to make a hook through the thick country to the east of Kuala Kangsar and advance on the town of Ipoh. On 26th December the regiment crossed the river unopposed and headed south with all speed. Yamashita was concerned, however, about the obstacle presented by the stretch of country between Kampat and Kuala Kubu. Here both the road and railway ran through a narrow defile, giving no opportunity for flanking movements except by sea. In the hands of a stubborn enemy, the defile could be blocked for weeks on end, and the momentum of the Japanese advance could be lost. What were the best tactics to be adopted? Yamashita's appreciation was that the British and Indian troops were in such a state that stiff resistance could only be offered by them at long intervals. So he must keep hustling them, keep pushing one body of troops through another so that there was no let-up. His orders were, therefore, that once the Guards had taken Ipoh, Matsui should go through and head for Kuala Lumpur, the large city and administrative centre in Selangor. While this move was in the early stages, 4th Guards Regiment would carry out a lightning move via Bentong to cut off the British retreat. Yamashita was angry at the way his junior commanders kept letting the enemy troops slip away at night. 'I don't just want them pushed back,' he kept repeating, 'I want them destroyed.' So far his line of communications was working fairly well, though there was already a shortage of artillery ammunition. As he realised only too well, every mile he advanced meant extra stress on communications and he was still hundreds of miles from Singapore.

During the next few days he moved forward rapidly, and by 31st December III Corps was back at Kampar, some twenty-five miles to the south of Ipoh. Here General Heath hoped to halt the Japanese, for the position was a strong one, laying either side of a steep jungle-clad hill. For the infantry there was a field of fire of over a thousand yards – a great relief after

Black smoke from burning rubber supplies: valuable war material was denied to the advancing enemy

Above: Many Chinese joined the Royal Army Medical Corps. *Below:* Indian reinforcements reach Singapore. Their uniforms, like their training, were for desert warfare

the country through which they had fought so far. Artillery observation was good also and there was a hope that at last the gunners could tip the balance against the Japanese. Matsui's plan was to attack down the road, while 42nd Regiment made a detour to the west. In fact the latter unit found itself floundering in swamp and was too late to influence the battle.

This opened just after dawn on New Year's Day 1942. The Japanese guns and mortars opened up, plastering the forward positions before Kampar. As the guns lifted the infantry rushed in and heavy fighting broke out. They were held, except on the right where they captured a feature known as Thompson's Ridge and altogether the situation looked reasonably stable. Some of the British and Indian troops put up the best showing they had made so far. To quote Percival:

'The (enemy) attacks were made with all the well-known bravery and disregard of danger of the Japanese soldier. There was the dogged resistance in spite of heavy losses, by

the men of the British Battalion and their supporting artillery, and finally, when the enemy had captured a key position and the battalion reserves were exhausted, there was a charge in the old traditional style by the Sikh company of the 1/8th Punjab Regiment. Through a tremendous barrage of mortar and machine-gun fire they went, led by their company commander, Captain Graham, until he fell mortally wounded, and then by their subedar. Their cheering rose to a roar as they charged, routing the enemy with heavy loss. The situation was completely restored, but only 30 of this gallant company remained. The battle of Kampar had proved that our trained troops, whether they were British or Indian, were superior man for man to the Japanese troops.'

But troops need commanders and equipment, and commanders need confidence in their own ability to dominate events. Before nightfall General Heath received news that a Japanese sea-borne force had landed some twenty miles further south at Utan Melintang and was making its way inland. 12th Brigade were ordered to keep it away from the trunk road but meanwhile Major-General Paris (who had replaced Murray-Lyon as commander 11th Division) became worred about his line of communications and asked permission to withdraw. Heath approached Percival, who eventually agreed, but insisted that 11th Division must go on fighting in the defile and keep the enemy north of Kuala Kubu – eighty miles below Kampar – until 15th January. Once Kuala Kubu went, Kuantan airfield would go with it, and if this happened before the promised convoy had reached Singapore there would only be further disaster.

In fact, on 3rd January, as 11th Division was withdrawing from Kampar, a convoy carrying 45th Indian Brigade reached Singapore in safety. But the news was not so good as it sounded. When Percival saw the troops he found them 'very young, unseasoned and undertrained, and straight off the ship after their first experience of the sea'. The reinforcements to follow them would not be much better, and some would be even worse.

Wavell takes command

On Christmas Day 1941 there was a conference of the Chiefs of Staff at the White House. Here the American Army Chief of Staff, General Marshall, proposed that a Supreme Commander should be appointed for the Far East and, after further discussion, the name of General Sir Archibald Wavell was put forward. The British Chiefs of Staff were not very happy about the idea, fearing the results of public opinion in America if further disasters occurred, and they seemed inevitable. Wavell probably had a greater reputation than any British general at this time. He had won a fine victory over the Italians in the Libyan desert – the first British military victory of the war – but later had been overwhelmed by events in the Mediterranean Command, and transferred to India where he became Commander-in-Chief. A dry, unflamboyant Scot, Wavell was liked by troops and subordinate commanders alike and was a soldier of great ability. Dr Johnson once said of Oliver Goldsmith that 'he writes like an angel and speaks like poor poll' and to some extent this comment applied to Wavell too. His prose was supple and lucid, and he had a great narrative gift. Among British generals he could only be matched as a writer by Sir Ian Hamilton, the commander at Gallipoli. But as a lecturer or speaker he was somewhat pathetic. Like Hamilton he had an unlucky streak in action and often seemed to arrive on the scene when the situation was desperate. His new command was known as ABDA – the initials stood for American, British, Dutch and Australian – and stretched from Burma to the Philippines. It is not surprising that on being informed of the appointment he commented, 'I have heard of men having to hold the baby but this is twins'. Lieutenant-General Sir Henry Pownall, who had replaced Brooke-Popham (on Duff Cooper's insistence) would become his chief of staff, and the old Headquarters Far East was abolished.

But appointing new commanders does not produce immediate divi-

General Sir Archibald Wavell

dends, any more than reorganising units. It was 7th January before Wavell reached Singapore and by that time there had been new disasters.

On 1st January the Japanese struck at 22nd Indian Brigade (of General Barstow's 9th Division) and pushed them off the airfield at Kuantan, which lies on the east coast, some 160 miles to the north of Singapore. The enemy land-based aircraft took a giant step towards their final objective.

Meanwhile 11th Division had gone back to the only obstacle before Kuala Lumpur – the Slim River. Here its task, laid down by Percival, was to keep the enemy north of Kuala Lumpur till 14th January, and longer if possible. Naturally, General Heath was worried by the possibility of further Japanese landings down the coast, especially at Kuala Selangor and Port Swettenham where there was an excellent harbour. To meet this threat he detached a mixed force of cavalry and infantry, supported by a battery of guns.

In fact, Yamashita had just given out new orders which involved a seaborne landing behind the British. Matsui and 5th Division, reinforced by a tank battalion, would advance direct on Kuala Lumpur, while detachments from the Guards Division landed at the ports just mentioned. When these arrived, however, on 2nd January, they met a hot reception from the gunners and failed to land that day, or on the 3rd. On the 4th, however, they secured a foothold north of Kuala Selangor, and after a sharp battle pushed inland in battalion strength. Urgently Percival called on the Royal Navy to stop any further landings, but the Perak Flotilla, which had been organised to meet this kind of threat, was down to two motor launches. Again the overwhelming superiority of the Japanese air arm was making its impact. By day the Flotilla was bombed so mercilessly that it could only shelter in the creeks, and when it came out at night, it was too late to catch the enemy seaborne forces. So the army had to cope as best it could.

While this was happening, 11th Division tried to fortify its new positions covering the Slim River. These covered the road and railway lines, and it was thought that the jungle on the flanks was so thick and cluttered with undergrowth that the Japanese could not possibly carry out another of their hooks. Apart from the road itself, which was mined, the position also was thought to be tank proof.

But the trouble was that the men could not work during the day because of the increased bombing and machine gunning from the air, so digging could only take place in darkness. Though the bombing did not inflict many casualties, it robbed the troops of sleep and its demoralising effect was considerable. The commanding officer of 5/2nd Punjab wrote of this time:

'The battalion was dead tired; most of all the Commanders, whose responsibilities prevented them from snatching even a little fitful sleep. The battalion had withdrawn 176 miles in three weeks and had had only three days' rest. It had suffered 250 casualties of which a high proportion had been killed. The spirit of the men was low, and the battalion had lost 50 per cent of its fighting efficiency.'

And of 5th January, he wrote:

'I found a most lethargic lot of men who seemed to want to do nothing but sit in slit trenches. They said they could not sleep because of the continued enemy air attacks. In fact, they were thoroughly depressed. There was no movement on the road, and the deadly ground silence emphasized by the blanketing effect of the jungle was getting on the men's nerves . . . The jungle gave the men a blind feeling.'

It was this day that the Japanese launched their attack. Soon they came under heavy fire from the 4/19th Hyderabad and retired, leaving sixty dead on the field. After midnight they attacked again, down both the railway and the road. Then, as the moon came up after 0300 hours, put down a series of artillery concentrations and sent a tank column down the road, followed by lorried infantry. Within an hour the first road block had been dealt with, and the tanks moved on again till the leader stuck a mine in front of the Punjabis', by Milestone

61. Immediately the infantry leaped out of the trucks and came at the Punjabis who fought them with rifles and light machine guns, and later with the bayonet. Three tanks were put out of action. Then the Japanese discovered some loop roads which, though overgrown with bushes, were still usable, and pushed the tanks round them, on to Milestone 62 where they bumped the Punjabi's Reserve Company. Of the fight which followed, Colonel Deakin of the Punjabi's has written:

'The din . . . baffles description. The tanks were head to tail, engines roaring, crews screaming, machine-guns spitting, and mortars and cannon firing all out. The platoon astride the cutting threw grenades, and one tank had its track smashed by anti-tank rifles. The two anti-tank guns fired two rounds one of which scored a bull, and then retired to the Argyll's area. One more tank wrecked itself on the mines.'

For a whole hour the reserve company and battalion headquarters held the fury of the attack, though not without taking heavy casualties. Then at 0630 hours the Japanese discovered the second loop road and moved on again. By this time they had thirty tanks in action.

The gallant defence of the Punjabis against great odds should have given the units behind them ample time to block and mine the road, but again there was muddle and confusion and the telephone lines were cut. The Argyll and Sutherland Highlanders just had time to put up one block where the trunk road ran through a rubber estate, when four medium tanks came down the road and swept it aside. Now the tanks went on to Trolak, some six miles north of the Slim River bridge, where they were temporarily halted by the Argyll's armoured cars, armed, incredibly, with only anti-tank rifles. Before long, however, the inevitable happened; the armoured cars were knocked out and the Argylls had to take cover and watch helplessly as the tanks swept on. Again, those responsible for blowing the bridge had failed in their duty. Eventually the Scots made their way back to the Slim River through the jungle.

General Sir Henry Pownall: at the last minute he took over from Brooke-Popham

Meanwhile the Japanese tanks had gone on, catching 5/14th Punjab as it moved forward to occupy a check position. The leading companies lost heavily before they had time to scramble into the jungle. Here they were joined by the rear companies and fired onto the road. Soon the tanks were joined by lorried infantry and a battle developed. The Japanese, with the support of the tanks, gradually got the upper hand, and yet another battalion had to make its way back to the Slim River through the jungle. The anti-tank guns, which had been sent forward to support the Punjabis in their check position, were overrun before they could even come into action.

What brought the Japanese success, apart from the great advantage of possessing tanks, was the incredible speed with which they launched their attacks. Any unit which was caught off-guard or out of position was scattered and overwhelmed in a matter of minutes. Time and again 11th Division was caught by events, not only because of exhaustion but because of bad communications. In the series of retreats from Jitra most of the radio equipment had been lost, and in any case, the art of using radios in thick country had not yet been mastered. Telephone lines were frequently cut, and by the time runners

Milestone 61 Milestone 62 Trolak Check Position

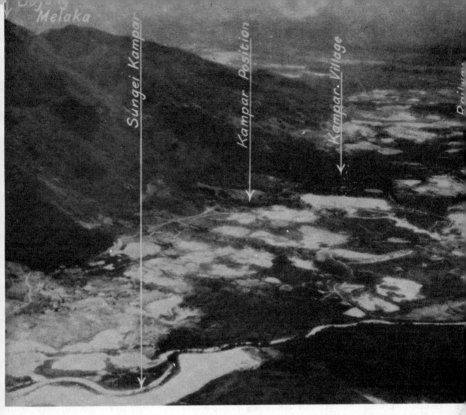

had got through with messages, the situation had changed – always for the worse. The tanks kept going. They passed straight through the 2/9th Gurkhas who were moving into position at Kampon Slim, a village about six miles before the river bridge. The troops stayed where they were, to await the attack by infantry. Further down the road, however, the tanks caught 2/1st Gurkhas advancing in column of route and quickly scattered them, then shot up two batteries of 137th Field Regiment, parked by the road, before heading for the Slim River Bridge which they reached soon after 0830 hours.

Here the only unit was a troop of Bofors anti-aircraft guns, and its commander, fortunately warned by a signaller who raced back in a truck, brought down his sights and opened fire on the tanks at a hundred yards range. It was quite useless. The small shells bounced off the tanks' hulls, and the Japanese took a heavy toll of the Bofors gunners, who were soon scattered. The tanks went over the bridge, leaving one of their number to guard it, and continued down the road another two miles. Now they came across the 155th Field Regiment, RA whose gunners had no idea that there were enemy tanks within twenty miles. Rapidly getting over their surprise they struggled to get their guns into action, and a 4.5-inch howitzer scored a direct hit on the leading tank at a range of thirty yards. This brought the advance to an end and, harrassed by tank-hunting parties, the Japanese concentrated their armour on the bridge, where they came under heavy fire from 155th Field Regiment. But they had done a magnificent job disorganising almost two brigades and robbing the British of large quantities of guns and transport. The British Official War History describes the action as 'a major disaster' and this is no exaggeration. The British losses led to the abandonment of central Malaya, and reduced the chances of holding on to Johore until reinforce-

The Japanese secret weapon,
the bicycle, which could be used on
jungle paths as well as roads

ments could be brought into the battle. That the regiments fought badly cannot be denied, but so would most units caught by armour when moving in close formation along a road. There was obviously a complete lack of training on how to deal with tanks, and especially on the use of anti-tank guns in country like Malaya but in 1941 infantry were simply not equipped to deal with tanks.

It was while the Slim River action was going on that Wavell arrived in Singapore to take command. From the first he realised that what he needed more than anything was time: time to establish a string of air-bases from Singapore to Java; time to land 18th British Division at Singapore, and, if possible a fresh Australian corps. Somehow, if this were to be done, the enemy must be held north of Johore until the end of January.

But first he wanted to inspect the troops and find out what was wrong with them, so he headed north to see Heath and Gordon Bennett. The Australian commander Bennett was a controversial character, highly critical of everything British and almost anyone put over him. He had not yet led his troops into action. Many of these had arrived in Singapore completely untrained – as he put it: 'They were recruited on a Friday and were put on a boat for Malaya the following week'. Some of them on disembarkation did not even know how to fire their rifles. However, as the division had not yet been in action, there was time to do some jungle training and Bennett seemed confident that he could stop the Japanese if no one else could. Now he would be put to the test, for Wavell's orders were that he should take up a position along the Muar River. Heath's III Corps, which could obviously not hold out before Kuala Lumpur for more than two more days, would withdraw through his lines, and after refitting, take up position on the east and west coasts of Johore. The plan had disadvantages, allowing Yamashita to advance without opposition through Selangor, Negri Sembilan and Malacca, but he realised that there was no point in trying to keep 11th Division in action any longer. It had completely shot its bolt.

Having given out his orders, Wavell returned to Singapore, where another shock was awaiting him, almost as great as the news from Slim River. Questioning Brigadier Ivon Simson, the senior Sapper officer on the island, he found that the latter's suggestions that defence works should be started had been turned down by Percival. Furthermore, he had now been taken away from his job to run Civil Defence. Thinking that perhaps Simson might be exaggerating, or trying to work off an old grudge against Percival, Wavell sent for him, and the two generals made a tour of the north shore of the island. It was now that Wavell realised for the first time that nothing had been done at all; that the shore was utterly defenceless. No works were even planned. 'Very much shaken' – to use his own words – he turned to Percival and angrily demanded why Simson's advice had not been taken and why nothing had been done. Percival's reply was that the construction of defence works would have a bad impact on morale. Hardly able to believe his ears, Wavell retorted that the impact would be even greater when the troops began crossing the causeway from the mainland, and by the look of things it would start happening before very long. With this he ordered Percival to set matters in hand at once.

Before leaving, Wavell had a session with Duff Cooper, who now felt that he had no job left and wanted to get away. A few days later his request was granted, but before leaving he signalled Churchill that there existed 'a widespread and profound lack of confidence in the administration' and added that, as a breakdown might paralyse the fighting services, some major changes were necessary. The result was that Stanley Jones, the much detested Colonial Secretary was sacked, while Sir Shenton Thomas remained where he was. A few days later, in a desparate bid to restore confidence, the latter declared in a circular to the Malay Civil Service:

'The day of minute papers has gone. There must be no more passing of files from one department to another, and from one officer in a department to another.'

To this the *Straits Times* commented sharply, 'The announcement is about two and a half years too

late'. The Malayan malaise was still as enervating as ever and reality had not even begun to break in. When a young officer commanding a detachment of ambulances drove up to the bungalow on a rubber plantation near Kuala Lumpur, the manager appeared, asking angrily how he dared to trespass on private property. A formal complaint would be sent in, he added, of a breach of regulations. The young officer replied that he would be leaving soon, as the Japanese would be arriving. Perhaps they would listen to the manager's complaints.

On 13th January a second convoy reached Singapore, bringing the British 18th Division, and fifty-one Hurrican fighters, still in crates. A week later, when the Japanese bombers came over, eight of them were shot down. But the Hurricanes proved no match for the Zeros, except at heights of over 20,000 feet, and the Zeros had no wish to go that high. So even with new men and material the situation still worsened. The British generals could only think of retreat, and everything now depended on Gordon Bennett and the Australians.

It might be imagined that, as his advance was going rapidly and at such little cost, Yamashita might have been highly delighted with himself, but his diary indicates otherwise. By now he suspected that when Singapore had fallen Tojo planned to kill him: though on what grounds it is not quite clear. Perhaps reports had reached him from home of the ecstatic press coverage given to his campaign. Since Homma was bogged down in the Philippines, the newspapers were writing up Malaya for all they were worth and Yamashita had become a national hero. As he realised only too well, Tojo feared and detested rivals and Yamashita had been too deeply involved in the business of assassination himself to doubt that Tojo would hesitate to put him out of the way. Relations with his old enemy, Field-Marshal Terauchi, had deteriorated too, and on 1st January Yamashita wrote in his diary: 'I can't rely on communications with Terauchi and Southern Army, or on air support from them. It is bad that Japan has no one in high places that

Above: Japanese infantry move forward under cover of the tanks. *Below left:* The advance on Kuala Lumpur. *Below right:* A British soldier surrenders: no more fighting, but his troubles were just beginning

can be relied upon. Most men abuse their power'. The following day he added: 'I dislike the selfishness of men in power. They have no conscience and their only aim is to grab even more power'. Yamashita had always hated rich civilians, especially those near the seat of government and on 5th was writing about the opportunists in Tokyo: 'These men pressed into national service are seldom any good in a crisis. Both civilian and military officers abuse their powers. I shall have to watch them'. The military officers were, of course, his old enemies in the Control Faction and the civilians the industrialists.

If his superiors did not win Yamashita's approval, his subordinates did little better, Of Nishimura, commander of the Imperial Guards Division, he wrote, 'He has wasted a week by disobeying orders', and even Matsui's 5th Division, which had carried the burden of the campaign, earned no praise. On the 6th Yamashita was writing: 'On the 6th I ordered them to carry out a flanking movement and so trap the enemy and crush him. But my orders weren't obeyed. I am disgusted with the lack of training and inferior quality of my commanders'. On the 8th he even wrote: 'The battalion commanders and troops lack fighting spirit. They've no idea how to *crush* the enemy.' Probably he was again harping on the fact that 11th Division kept getting away.

Though Yamashita was a perfectionist, there is no doubt that many of his remarks were justified. Many of the Japanese troops were badly trained; they chattered as they moved through the jungle; they lost their way; many officers and men were bad at map reading; co-ordination between infantry and gunners was sometimes primitive; and their standard of patrolling was weak. Lieutenant-Colonel Spencer Chapman, who was to stay in the jungles to organise guerilla warfare (now it was far too late Percival had agreed to this suggestion), watched the Japanese advancing towards Kula Lumpur:

'The majority were on bicycles in parties of forty or fifty, riding three or four abreast and talking and laughing just as if they were going to a football match. Indeed, some of them

were actually wearing football jerseys; they seemed to have no standard uniform or equipment and were travelling as light as they possibly could.'

The ordinary bicycle, in fact, was one of the Japanese army's secret weapons, for astride it a man could ride twenty miles or more a day with a rifle or light machine gun, ammunition and up to sixty pounds weight of equipment. When a unit came to a river, the men put the bicycles on their backs and waded across. By

this simple method the incredible momentum of the advance was maintained. And because of the overwhelming superiority in aircraft and tanks, many units had still not been in action, and part of Renya Mutaguchi's 18th Division had not even come south of the Thailand border.

Like all army commanders, Yamashita did not welcome visitors to his headquarters and on the 9th he wrote: 'Five staff officers have arrived from GHQ Tokyo. I hate them'. In fact, the

Kuala Lumpur: the street fighting begins

nearer he drew to Singapore, the more he was harassed by Tokyo and Southern Army Headquarters. Then Terauchi deliberately insulted him by issuing decorations to Major-General Takumi and his brigade group without prior consultation. Yamashita was incensed and wrote in his diary:

'If Southern Army is going to hand out the awards, men will take their orders from that formation and not from Twenty-fifth Army. That bloody Terauchi! He's living in luxury in Saigon with a comfortable bed, good food and playing Japanese chess.'

As the month of January wore on, Yamashita's neurosis grew more and more pronounced, and on one occasion his chief of staff, Suzuki recorded that 'Our general is near to mental explosion'.

Meanwhile, to cheer him, he had the spoils from Kuala Lumpur. Much of the reserve stocks had been moved back by rail, together with the supplies. Petrol and oil supplies were run to waste or fired and the airfield buildings were destroyed. Nevertheless, Kuala Lumpur was a huge prize and many stores were found intact.

On the day that his leading troops entered the town, Yamashita made a new appreciation. The last defensive position before Singapore, he thought, was the line of the Sungei Muar, and here he believed the British would

make a desperate effort to halt him. In view of this his plan was to concentrate the Imperial Guards Division at Malacca, where they would prepare to move down the coast. Meanwhile, after a rest, Mutsui's 5th Division would continue down the trunk road. In other words, his tactics were to keep outflanking the British positions while engaging them frontally at the same time. Also he asked Southern Army to land the remaining units of 18th Division at Singora and then send them to Johore by road. While this was happening, he ordered 55th Regiment to advance down the east coast to occupy Endau and Mersing. The plan was a good one given air superiority. Whether it would enjoy the swift success of the plans which had preceded it depended on Gordon Bennett and the Australians.

Australians in Bren gun carriers: the carriers were not a great success

Retreat to the island

Bennett's theory, which he had long propounded to Percival and Heath, was that the Japanese could be halted by a series of ambushes. The trunk road near Gemas, where his division (with 9th Indian Division in their rear) was now situated seemed ideal for the purpose, and so he laid his plans. A company of infantry was concealed in the jungle to the east of a river bridge, while a battery of field guns covered the road from the west. About tea-time Mukaide Detachment (a battalion of infantry on bicycles, supported by a tank regiment, some guns and sappers) came down the road and was allowed to pass. Then the bridge was blown and the infantry opened fire. Again communications with the gunners failed, so they did not open fire, but large numbers of Japanese were killed.

Next morning enemy bombers hit Gemas, and the Australian infantry posts a few miles west of the town came under attack, and again an ambush paid dividends. Several tanks were destroyed and the Japanese received eighty casualties. As more and more reinforcements came forward to join the battle, however, the Australians had to give some ground. On the 15th the RAF Buffalo fighters made a sortie, shooting up traffic heading for Gemas, and altogether the situation looked slightly more promising.

Hearing of the heavy losses in Mukaide Detachment, Matsui took control, sending 9th Infantry Brigade down the trunk road with orders to wipe out resistance before Batu Anam. Meanwhile he sent 21st Brigade on a wide sweep to the west of Mount Ophir. Pressure was also being exerted by the Imperial Guards Division who were moving down the coastal region in two columns. Nishimura's plan was to pin down the enemy in Muar town with one regiment, while another crossed the Sungei Muar higher up. It might be mentioned here that although relations between Yamashita and Nishimura had by no means improved during the campaign, the Imperial Guards Division had done far better than anticipated. Nishimura, a stubborn character, still went about things in his own way, interpreting his orders some-

what loosely, but while he was winning action after action, Yamashita did not interfere more than necessary.

In the action on the Sungei Muar, Nishimura was in luck, for his opponent was 11th Indian Brigade which had only just arrived and had not been into battle before. Its commander, Brigadier Duncan, was handicapped too, by orders from Gordon Bennett, who had made the same mistake as Murray-Lyon at Jitra – trying to cover every conceivable approach and therefore dispersing his troops far too widely. So, on 15th January, after the town of Muar had been bombarded for four days, the forward companies of the Rajputana Rifles, down by the coast near Kesang, were overrun. Then, after nightfall, a Guards battalion crossed the river in small craft and moved on Muar, surprising more Indian troops en route. Some of these were resting with their arms piled. Next day a frontal attack on Muar was foiled by 65th Australian battery who fired at the oncoming craft over open sights, but in the afternoon an attack from the east by the troops who had crossed higher up the Sungei Muar succeeded, and the remnants of the Rajputana Rifles withdrew. In two days' fighting they had lost their commanding officer and second-in-command plus hundreds of casualties. They had been completely outnumbered and outfought.

When news reached Bennett of events at Muar, he became concerned with his line of communications running back from Gemas, so despatched a battalion from 27th Australian Brigade to reinforce 45th Indian Brigade. His Intelligence, however, was wildly inaccurate, and he imagined that only a minor setback had been suffered at Muar. When briefing the commanding officer of the Australian battalion, he even remarked that 'The enemy strength is only about 200. You should be able to restore the situation with a counterattack, and get back to Gemas in a few days' time.' He seemed to have no idea that Nishimura with his whole division was moving down the coast.

Nishimura, however, having crossed the Sungei Muar far more easily than he had expected, now planned to trap and annihilate the enemy facing him, between the Sungei Muar and the Sungei Bat Pahat, thirty miles to the south-east. So he ordered 5th Guards Regiment to attack Bakri, while 4th Guards Regiment moved along the coast road, crossed the Sungei Bat Pahat north of the town, and held the road running inland to Bukit Pelandok. The attack went in at dawn on the 18th, and though the Indians and Australians held on grimly, they were outnumbered and eventually had to go back.

It was on the 18th too, that Percival tumbled to Yamashita's plan of pushing 5th Division down the road and the Imperial Guards Division down the coast. Against opposition from Bennett, he transferred the troops on the coast to Heath's command (labelling them Westforce) while Bennett's formations were called Eastforce. But the labels did not greatly help the situation. As Nishimura pushed on down the coast, Percival was increasingly worried about the threat to Bennett's rear, and so again the policy was retreat. There was no thought of getting behind the Japanese to cut their tenuous communications, no thought of any offensive action at all. Meanwhile 45th Brigade at Parit Sulong was cut off and its wounded were lying in the open, many of them dying for want of medical attention. On 22nd January two aircraft from Singapore were able to drop food and medical supplies to the beleaguered garrison. But the situation was growing desperate. When a counterattack by an Australian unit failed to provide any relief, Lieutenant-Colonel Anderson decided to get the brigade out as best he could. Ordering all heavy equipment and ammunition reserves to be destroyed and leaving the wounded behind under the charge of volunteers, he ordered the units to break up and make their way through the jungle in small parties. Eventually 500 Australians and 400 Indians, many of them wounded, succeeded in getting back, But as a fighting unit the brigade had been destroyed.

By this time Matsui's troops had reached Labis on the trunk road and he decided to stick to the coastal

Left: A street in Johore : Japanese infantry wait while the tank knocks out machine gun positions. *Above:* The attack on Gemas railway station

road and head for Batu Pahat. Once this town had been reduced, he would be within eighty miles of Singapore.

Singapore began to occupy the thoughts of many people at this time, not least Winston Churchill and the Allied leaders. On 15th January Churchill wrote to Wavell:

'Please let me know your idea of what would happen in the event of your being forced to withdraw into the island.

How many troops would be needed to defend this area? What means are there of stopping landings [such] as were made in Hong Kong?'

On the following day Wavell replied that during his first visit to the island he found that all the plans were based on the need for repulsing a sea-borne attack, and the situation was 'that little or nothing was done to construct defences on north side of island to prevent crossing Johore Straits . . .' The news came as a staggering blow to Churchill who later was to write:

'It was with feeling of painful surprise that I read this message on the morning of the 19th. So there were no permanent fortifications covering the landward side of the naval base and of the city! Moreover, even more astounding, no measures worth speaking of had been taken by any of the commanders since the war began, and more especially since the Japanese had established themselves in Indo-China, to construct field defences . . . I cannot understand how it was I did not know this. But none of the officers on the spot and none of my professional advisers at home seem to have realised this awful need . . . I do not write this in any way to excuse myself. I ought to have known. My advisers ought to have known and I ought to have been told, and I ought to have asked.'

The reason he did not ask, Churchill explains, was that the possibility of Singapore island having no landward defences 'no more entered into my mind than that of a battleship being launched without a bottom.'

But this indeed was the situation. And the excuses given to Churchill were the same as had been given to Brigadier Ivan Simson when he had

105

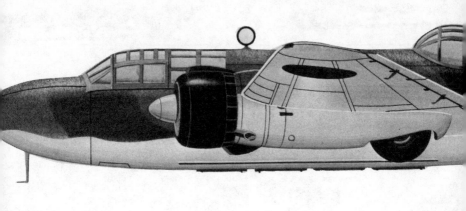

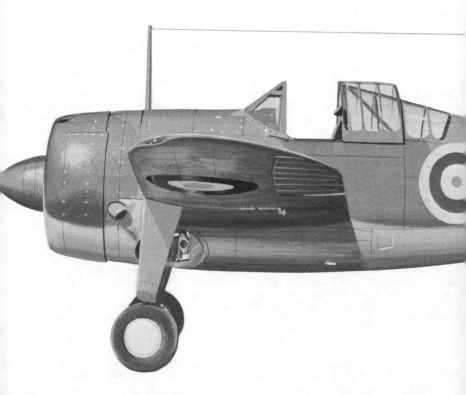

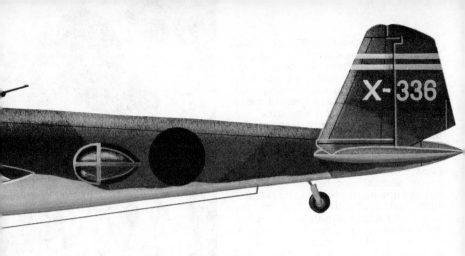

Mitsubishi G3M2 (Navy Type 96 Attack Bomber Model 22) Allied code name 'Nell'
Engines: Two Mitsubishi *Kinsei* 45 radials, 1,075 hp at take off. *Defensive armament:* One 20mm Type 99 Mk I cannon and four 7.7mm Type 92 machine guns. *Bomb load:* 1,764 lbs. *Maximum speed:* 232 mph at 13,715 feet. *Ceiling:* 29,950 feet. *Range:* 2,722 miles. *Span:* 82 feet $0\frac{1}{4}$ inch. *Length:* 53 feet $11\frac{5}{8}$ inches

Thought by the Allies to be capable of besting the Japanese aircraft by which it would be opposed, the *Brewster F2A Buffalo* was in fact inferior in every respect except strength and pilot and fuel protection to the Mitsubishi Zero. *Engine:* Wright R-1820, 940 hp. *Armament:* Four .5-inch machine guns and two 100-lb. bombs. *Maximum speed:* 301 mph at 17,000 feet. *Climb rate:* 3,060 feet per minute. *Ceiling:* 32,500 feet. *Range:* 1,095 miles. *Weight empty:* 3,785 lbs. *Weight loaded:* 5,370 lbs. *Span:* 35 feet. *Length:* 26 feet

first raised the matter. The fact that troops had to concentrate on training, lack of funds from Whitehall, the effort to build defences in northern Malaya. To this Churchill commented: 'I do not consider these reasons valid. Defences should have been built.'

But with the enemy less than a hundred miles away and coming on fast, what was to be done? On the 19th, Churchill wrote to General Ismay, Chief of Staff, that an emergency plan should be made at once by attempting to use the fortress guns with reduced charges, by mining and obstructing landing places, by wiring and booby-traps, by constructing field works at strong points, by planting field batteries with searchlights at each end of the Straits. He added: 'The entire male population should be employed upon constructing defence works . . . the defence of Singapore Island must be maintained by every means . . . the city of Singapore must be converted into a citadel and defended to the death. No surrender can be contemplated.'

On the 20th Churchill signalled to Wavell:

'I want to make it absolutely clear that I expect every inch of ground to be defended, every scrap of material or defences to be blown to pieces to prevent capture by the enemy, and no question of surrender to be entertained until after protracted fighting among the ruins of Singapore City.'

It was significant that the word 'surrender' had now been mentioned for the first time. This message crossed with a signal from Wavell who, while assuring Churchill that Percival had orders to hold out as long as possible, added:

'I must warn you however that I doubt whether island can be held long when Johore is lost . . . Part of garrison had been sent into Johore, and many troops remaining are doubtful value. I am sorry to give you depressing picture, but I do not want you to have false picture of island fortress.'

The following day, 20th January, Wavell signalled again, advising that the situation had greatly deteriorated, and 'will necessitate withdrawal of troops in Segamat-Labis area, and may necessitate general withdrawal towards Johore, Bahru, and even-

tually to island.' Preparatory measures for the defence of the island, he added, were being put in hand with the limited resources available. The viability of the defence, however, would depend not only on the state of the troops, but 'the ability of Air Force to maintain fighters on Island.' Though he did not add this, the RAF had only twenty-eight fighters left and so were hopelessly outnumbered.

His statement regarding 'preparatory measures' for the defence of Singapore proved something of an exaggeration. Although Wavell had been urging Percival on, virtually nothing at all was done till 23rd January when an outline plan was issued, and it was another five days before details went out. By this time the civilian labour force had been scattered by the incessant air raids, and when the call went out, very few

The Australians have met the enemy:
Gordon Bennett with war
correspondents

came forward to answer it. Not a
spade was thrust into the earth until
the end of the month.

As long as military history is
written, there will be speculation on
this fantastic situation. Why did it
not occur to anyone to build defences
on the northern shore when the base
was planned in the 1920s and 1930s?
Why did no one react to General
Dobbie's warning that the Japanese
could come down the peninsula? Why
did not Percival respond to the
danger – and more especially why did
he take no notice whatever of Brigadier Simson's warning? Why did he
not obey Wavell's orders (or 'urgings',
as the Official War History puts it)?
How could a man who was so gallant
in action and sane about other
matters, be inept to the borders of
insanity in this one? Why should
civilian morale have so dominated his

thoughts to the extent that military
necessity was ignored? His own
account in *The War in Malaya* has a
kind of crazy logic about it and is
worth quoting:

'The fact that no defences had been
constructed on the north and west
coasts of the island . . . has been the
subject of much critical comment,
even in the highest quarters. It has
been imputed to a lack of foresight on
the part of successive officers commanding. Such criticism is most
unjust. In the first place, general
officers commanding had no authority
to construct defence when or where
they liked. The defences of Singapore
were built up in accordance with a
War Office plan . . . Then there was the

Johore: the battle of the roadblocks. *Above left:* An Australian anti-tank crew take on tanks at close quarters. *Above right and below:* The tanks burned and the crews did not all escape

Above left: As always the civilians suffered: after an air raid on a Malayan Kumpong. *Above right:* Impressive but useless: the guns on Singapore pointed the wrong way. *Below right:* Ack-Ack guns had occasional successes

question of the object of the defences. It was quite definitely the protection of the Naval Base – not the defence of Singapore Island.'

But how could the Naval base be protected once the enemy had been allowed to cross on to the island? To this he gives no acceptable answer. Altogether, one can only conclude that in this sphere Percival was as stupid as he was stubborn. Because everything had been done 'in accordance with a War Office plan', because the paper work had gone through and every procedure had been observed, he remained content. Percival simply did not respond to the realities of war.

His mind could not seem to grasp the fact that Yamashita's swift advance had blown previous theories sky high.

Curiously enough, while defending his own record for having done nothing, Percival compliments himself on what had been done, before the troops streamed over the Johore causeway:

'Sites for forward defended localities and for reserves had been selected. Artillery observation posts and gun positions had been reconnoitred. Locations of formations headquarters had been fixed and communications arranged. Machine-gun positions had been constructed. Oil obstacles and

depth charges had been placed in creeks which appeared to be likely landing places. Spare searchlights had been collected and made available. Anti-tank obstacles had been constructed . . . The general plan of defence was to cover the approaches with defended localities and to hold mobile reserves ready for counter-attack.'

To this one can only observe that these preparations sound much better on paper than they appeared to the troops. The defence plan would probably not have worked even without his own inept handling of the battle. But that is to anticipate. There were still the last battles to be fought on the Peninsula.

On the morning of 22nd January Percival held a conference at Regam during which he decided to fall back on a line running from Kluang to Ayer Hitam. This would mean that only the tip of the peninsula – twenty miles of it – would remain in Allied hands. The withdrawal went ahead untidily, hampered by bad communications and under heavy attack from the air. Frequently the infantry commanders called for air support, but with the RAF down to seventy-four bombers and twenty-eight fighters (the Japanese strength was 250 and 150 respectively) only one call could be dealt with at a time. However, attacks were made on Kuala Lumpur and Kuantan airfields and the bombers struck enemy transport on the trunk road. These efforts, however, made no impact on events whatsoever. Meanwhile the Japanese kept hammering away at towns and villages, damaging civilian morale. In January there were no less than 2,100 civilian casualties in Singapore city alone.

The retreat went on, delayed from time to time when regiments fought stubbornly, and junior commanders rose to the occasion. There was no lack of gallantry among either officers or men; they were simply outgunned and outfought, and however many tanks they destroyed, more and more were ready to come against them. The hammering from the air went on all through the hours of daylight. Away on the east coast, 22nd Australian Brigade scored a

minor success, ambushing 40th Infantry Regiment near Mersing. The Japanese were so heavily mauled that they began retiring and Yamashita sent strong reinforcements.

On 26th January Heath issued orders for III Corps to withdraw to Singapore Island.

But still there was to be another disaster. 22nd Indian Brigade was cut off by a Japanese encircling movement, and its commander, Brigadier Painter, decided that the only hope was to retreat through the jungle to the west of the railway. The units moved off, carrying their wounded, and for four days struggled to escape the enemy net. By now the formation was reduced to 350 men, almost without ammunition, and on 1st February when they came up against a strong Japanese position blocking their path, Painter had no option but to surrender. Only a few men, separated from the main body, gained the temporary haven of Singapore Island.

But to go back a few days: on 26th January Percival had signalled Wavell:

'Consider general situation becoming grave. With our depleted strength it is difficult to withstand enemy ground pressure combined with continuous and practically unopposed air activity. We are fighting all the way but may be driven back into the Island within a week.'

The next evening he wrote in a personal message:

'Very critical situation has developed. The enemy has cut off and overrun majority of forces on west coast . . . Unless we can stop him it will be difficult to get our own columns on other roads back in time especially as they are both being pressed. In any case it looks as if we should not be able to hold Johore for more than another three or four days. We are going to be a bit thin in the Island unless we can get all remaining troops back.'

The total fighter strength, he added, was down to nine, and it was becoming difficult to keep the airfields in action.

Wavell's view was that in this emergency all the troops should be evacuated from the mainland. It was certainly no use letting them get cut off there to gain one or two days. On 28th Percival held a conference at which Heath pointed out that neither Eastforce nor Westforce had any reserves left, and any attempt to cling on to southern Johore would mean further disaster. So it was decided that evacuation should begin as soon as possible, and be completed by the night of the 30th/31st. This decision was fortunate, for Yamashita had decided to send a column striking inland from the west coast to seal the retreat routes. If he could cut off all the troops in Johore, he believed, Singapore would surrender without a protracted struggle. His move very nearly succeeded.

The weary troops began streaming back over the 1,100 yard causeway between Johore and Singapore Island. Many, it is said, believed that their long nightmare was over, that the island was an impregnable fortress where they could hold out until a strong naval and military force came to relieve them. They were soon to be disillusioned. The island was not a fortress. The plan for its defence had only been brought out on 28th January; and civilians, even in this moment of crisis, were still trying to exercise their overriding privileges. When Major Angus Rose, of the Argyll and Sutherland Highlanders, decided to cut down some banana trees to improve his field of fire, he was told peremptorily that he must first get permission 'from the competent authority'; and when it was decided to make the Golf Club a strong point, the secretary there advised that 'nothing can be done till we've called a meeting of the committee'. And a gunner officer who sited his troops on the links was asked what on earth he was doing. Didn't he realise that the Golf Club was private property.

Apart from other considerations of command and morale, it was hardly likely that a battle begun in such an atmosphere of fantasy and frustration would go well. The augurs were correct. The campaign was now entering the last phase . . . the last and most disastrous of all.

The last action before Singapore: street fighting in Johore Bahru

**Prelude
to battle**

On 31st January Percival assumed command of all the troops on the island. They totalled some 85,000, but of this number 15,000 were administrative or non-combatant, so he had nearly the strength of three divisions. Of infantry, he had thirteen British battalions, six Australian, seventeen Indian and two Malay. There were also three machine gun battalions. On paper this looked a strong force but reality was somewhat different: six of the British battalions had only just come off the ships, and the other battalions were very much under strength. Every unit contained large numbers of men who were virtually little more than recruits. There was a terrible shortage of weapons, particularly among the units which had fought on the mainland, and only one of the three machine gun units was anything like complete.

But even worse than lack of weapons was the blow to morale when the men learned that not only were the remaining aircraft being flown out, but also that the Naval base had been evacuated. The latter was a staggering blow, for the base was what the campaign had been fought to defend. George Hammond of the *Malaya Tribune*, wrote later of his reaction to the news: 'Never throughout all the fighting – all the defeats – did I ever feel such a sense of utter dismay. It seemed impossible that this naval fortress which had cost £60 million and taken seventeen years to build could have been thrown away like this – without even a fight for it.' The base, it should be emphasised, was gigantic. It had oil tanks with a capacity of millions of tons, it had underground munition dumps, workshops, dry docks and graving docks. The floating dock was so huge that 60,000 men could stand on its bottom. There were twenty-two square miles of deep sea anchorage. There was a complete town to house several thousand men, complete with shops, cinemas, churches, and no less than seventeen football pitches. How had it come to be evacuated *before the troops had marched over the causeway* – the troops who had come to offer their lives in its defence? Who had given the orders?

Though the troops were never to

learn this, the Admiralty had warned Rear-Admiral Spooner, Naval Commander-in-Chief, as early as 21st January that he should get his skilled personnel away from the Base. A week later Spooner had transferred all the dockyard staff to Singapore city, then shipped most of them to Ceylon. The only men left behind were those detailed to give assistance to the army demolition units. Spooner did not even advise Percival that the carefully worked out 'scorched earth' scheme had not been carried out before his men left, and, if anything were to be done at all, the troops would have to act.

Learning the news, George Hammond and some other journalists motored out to the Base and the scene which met them was almost beyond belief. To quote Noel Barber's *Sinister Twilight:*

'Lolling Indian sentries at the gates waved them inside without bothering to enquire what they wanted. They walked past deserted barracks which had housed a labour force of 12,000 Asians; near the empty administration offices an acre of ground was littered with equipment – everything from shirts and truncheons to gas masks and wooden lockers. The great crane that could lift out an entire gun turret was still in working order; enormous ships boilers stood in the boiler shop awaiting the Japanese navy, together with lathes, spares for seaplanes, shelves of radio equipment, scores of boxes of valves; one warehouse was filled with huge coils of rope, wire or cord. In the causeway George could see the upper works of the giant floating dock that had been towed all the way from England.'

Everywhere remained signs of hasty departure or panic. A football lay still by the goal posts. Half finished meals littered the Mess Hall, and the galleys were crowded with pans, plates, and cutlery still unwashed after the last meal. Flies and rats had already moved in to locate the abandoned food and then truck-loads of troops arrived 'on the scrounge', many of them replacing shirts and trousers which had been worn to shreds on the retreat. They also were glad of the cigarettes and tinned food which were still available in huge quantities.

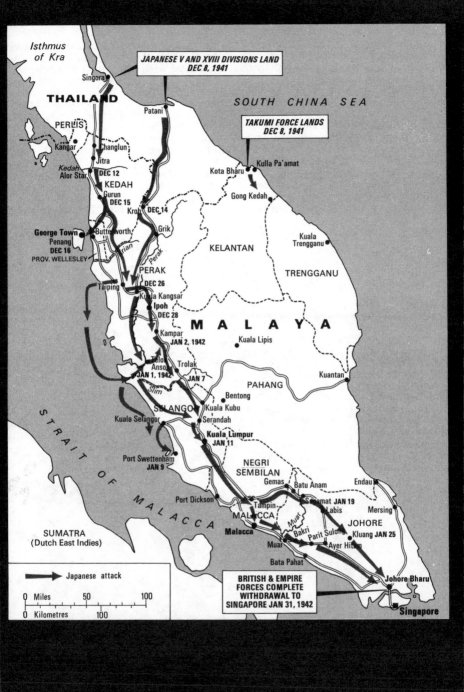

The army had to allocate 120 lorries each of which made twenty-one trips before all the portable gear left by the navy had been removed.

Hurriedly preparing for his last battle, Percival decided that the Japanese might combine their attack across the Johore Strait with a seaborne operation, and therefore decided that the whole seventy miles of coastline would have to be defended.

But what were to be the defensive tactics? To stop the Japanese landing and deal with them near the beaches, should they succeed? Or to hold the beaches thinly, holding the main forces available for counterattack? The second alternative would mean that the battle would have to be fought inland, in close country which would favour the Japanese. It also meant a steep drop in both civilian and military morale, once knowledge spread that the enemy were on the island. Percival therefore decided on the first alternative, though realising

Australian anti-tank gun in position covering the Johore causeway, with the Imperial Palace in the background

that the coastline, intersected with creeks and mangrove swamps would be difficult to defend, and that large stretches would be held lightly because of lack of troops.

But what was to be the command pattern? Percival decided to split the island into three areas – Northern, Southern and Western. Gordon Bennett's 8th Australian Division would be the major formation in the Western Area, running west from the causeway, while 11th and 18th Divisions would hold the Northern Area, which ran from the causeway east-wards. In Southern Area were a mixed bag of troops, including 1st Malaya Brigade. The plan can hardly be described as a good one, and contained one fatal flaw. During his visit to the island on 20th January, Wavell had warned Percival that the north-west coast presented the weak spot, and here Yamashita would be most likely to attack. Here, he suggested the 18th British Division – which though inexperienced was still fresh – should be sited. Percival, however, believed that the attack would come in from the north-east

British infantryman: not really at home in the conditions prevalent in Malaya, the British troops, many of them not fully trained, were no match for the Japanese, especially as they were not well or boldly led

and so disposed his troops accordingly. So the vital north-west sector was given to Gordon Bennett who had under him his own division (weakened by 1,900 untrained reinforcements) and 44th Indian Brigade, a formation that was partially trained and unsure of itself. Bennett was far from sure of himself too, and wrote:

'To hold the Australian front I have only four reliable infantry battalions and two companies of the well-trained machine-gun battalion. The area is the most uninhabited part of the island. I held a conference of brigade commanders . . . all agreed that we were undermanned. I realised the unfairness of asking them and their men to fight without resources . . . The northwest part of the island is thickly covered with timber, mostly rubber, with thick mangrove growing right down to the water's edge. The posts, which are many hundreds of yards apart, have a field of fire of only 200 yards.'

If the front was weak the rear was cluttered, for all the administrative units were located in their own formations. Though many of these had no real tasks to perform, their men were not allocated to infantry units or formed into patrols to cover the ground between defence posts. Security was appalling, and many Japanese agents were still using their radios to give information on the siting and moves of units. Tokyo Radio was able to give details of damage caused by bombing raids.

It was now that the policy of not constructing defence works paid its frightful dividends, for all civilian labour had disappeared and the troops had to start digging their own defences. The task was a difficult one, and it proved quite impossible to dig trenches down near the beaches, for the water oozed in. So breastworks had to be constructed protected by barbed wire and tons of anti-tank mines. Most of this work had to be done at night to avoid air attack, so valuable hours were lost. However, dumps were assembled in the forward area with ten days' reserve of food and ammunition. At the same time, plans were made to blow up the main magazines on the island. Petrol from stocks held on the airfields –

now that no aircraft were left to use it – was allowed to run waste in the creeks, but, with a complete lack of imagination, Percival made no plans to use it against the enemy. With the millions of gallons available, it should have been possible to create a barrier of fire right along the Johore Strait – and this indeed is what the Japanese expected to happen. Apart from some booby-traps designed to spread small amounts of burning oil in the north-eastern creeks, nothing was done. And as Percival's appreciation concerning enemy intentions was quite wrong, even the booby-traps proved useless.

It will be recalled that Percival's reason or excuse for the complete lack of defence works along the northern coast was the possible damage to civilian morale. Now morale was damaged by rumours that Singapore was not to be defended. The Chinese, who feared the arrival of Japanese troops more than anyone, were in a state of panic. There were no air raid shelters and as the Japanese bombers came over, the streets of Singapore would be crowded with people running hither and thither, having no idea what to do or where to go. After each raid was over, trucks would go round picking up the bodies, which would then be dumped into communal graves. As one writer has observed, it was like the Black Death all over again.

Observing the state of morale, Percival issued a statement to the press:

'The Battle of Malaya has come to an end, and the Battle of Singapore has started. For nearly two months our troops have fought an enemy on the mainland who has held the advantage of great air superiority and considerable freedom of movement by sea.

Our task has been to impose losses on the enemy and to gain time to enable the forces of the Allies to be concentrated for this struggle in the Far East. Today we stand beleaguered in our island fortress.

In carrying out this task we want the help of every man and woman in the fortress. There is work for all to do. Any enemy who sets foot in the fortress must be dealt with im-

Japanese infantryman: tough, hardy and well trained, he swept through Malaya and into the supposedly impregnable British fortress of Singapore with great speed and efficiency

mediately. The enemy within our gates must be ruthlessly weeded out. There must be no more loose talk and rumour-mongering. Our duty is clear. With firm resolve and fixed determination we shall win through.'

It is doubtful if this appeal had any great effect; both troops and civilians could see the demolitions, or preparations for them, going on and draw the logical conclusion that those at the top regarded the situation as hopeless.

If Percival's situation was desperate, Yamashita's was far from happy. Instead of devoting their energies to keeping open the long and tenuous line of communications, Southern Army were bombarding him with paper. On 23rd January Field-Marshal Terauchi even sent his Chief of Staff, Lieutenant-General Osamu Tsukada, with voluminous notes on how to capture Singapore, and to Yamashita's fury left after lunch without saying 'thank you'. Yamashita tore the notes into shreds, observing in his diary: 'Whenever there are two alternatives, Southern Army always insist on the wrong one.' Ammunition was short for the assault on Singapore, especially shells for the field guns, and very little was coming through. Though the Air Division were hammering away at Singapore, they seldom obeyed Yamashita's instructions, and many requests for air strikes were completely ignored.

However, preparations for the assault went ahead with all speed and Yamashita, from his headquarters in the Imperial Palace of the Sultan of Johore, could look across to the island, his last objective in the campaign. His three divisions had closed up now, and in the creeks facing Singapore he had assembled 200 collapsible launches, equipped with outboard motors, and 100 larger landing craft. Day after day the assault troops were carrying out embarkation and landing drill and nothing was being left to chance. The 4,000 men forming the first wave had all fought in China and were masters of sea-borne landings. Yamashita knew they would not fail him.

By 4th February the reconnaissances for the crossing and the subse-

Above: Johore Causeway, blown up by demolition squad. *Right:* The dockside after a bombing raid.

quent staff work had been completed, and the chief of staff, Suzuki, began drafting the orders. At 1100 hours on the 6th Yamashita summoned his divisional commanders to the Imperial Palace to receive these. Briefly his plan was that Nishimura's division would make a feint to the east on the evening of 7th February by landing on Palau Ubin Island opposite Changi. Then after dark on the 8th 5th and 18th Divisions, under Matsui and Mutaguchi respectively, would cross to the north-west corner of the island. Once they were established the Imperial Guards Division would follow. Matsui and Mutaguchi were delighted with the plan, but Nishimura understandably was not, feeling that the Guards had been insulted by being given a subsidiary role. It might be added here that Yamashita was not merely relying on the feint by the Guards Division to mislead Percival. Dummy camps had been erected on the mainland opposite

the Naval Base, and convoys of lorries were ordered to move east by daylight, then double back after dark to repeat the manoeuvre the following day.

There was nothing particularly original about this manoeuvre – Allenby had done the same thing in Palestine in 1918 – but it confirmed to Percival that his judgement was right. So Brigadier Ivan Simson, who had been stocking up dumps to the west of the causeway, found himself ordered to move them to the east. Simson was naturally horrified, for all his military experience told him that the attack would come in from the north-west. He was certain of it. For weeks he had been assembling mines, booby-traps, barbed wire, pickets, drums of petrol and other materials. However, Percival was in command and his orders had to be obeyed, so with great effort the dumps were moved east of the causeway by 5th February. That night, however, Percival received reports from Gordon Bennett that the Japanese were missing opposite his sector to the west. Percival gave orders that the dumps were to be moved back again. But there was no time.

Yamashita's artillery bombardment opened on the 5th, the main targets being the three northern airfields, the Naval Base, and main road junctions. On the 6th the bombardment continued, mainly directed against the north-east of the island, and the end of the causeway. A sixty-yard gap had now been blown in this, and in the railway bridge alongside it. But, as the Japanese found later on, the water by the gap was only four feet deep at low tide and their men could wade across. On the 7th there was more shelling, and that night a patrol was sent across to reconnoitre the coast between the Sungei Skudei and the Sungei Malayu, but did not penetrate far enough to locate the landing craft. They did however report troop concentrations in the rubber plantations, and said there was a good deal of traffic on the roads in the area. This information did not reach Percival's headquarters until 1530 hours the following afternoon – even now the situation was static, communications continued to be unbelievably bad. When Bennett asked for an aircraft to observe for his artillery, he was told that none was available, so put down unobserved fire in the areas mentioned by the patrol. It should have been obvious to everyone by now, even Percival, that the attack was imminent, and every gun should have been trained on the creeks to the north-west. But as usual, Percival was not around when

Chaos in Singapore city: the population was swollen by 500,000 refugees

wanted, and the assault craft were allowed to assemble and load without interference.

From first light on 8th February the Japanese aircraft came over, bombing and machine gunning the Australians in the Western Area. Then in the afternoon the guns opened up, and for nearly five hours shelled forward defences, headquarters and communications. At sunset, by which time all the telephone lines had been cut, there was a lull, to be followed by an even heavier bombardment. Percival's view, with which Bennett agreed for once, was that the shelling would go on for three or four days, so no orders were given for the gunners to put down concentrations on the creeks. Yet again Percival's instinct had led him astray, and in fact many of his decisions at this time seemed to make no sense whatever. Within a few hours, however, he was to receive a disagreeable surprise, and the forward infantry would be opening up on the first assault wave. The last battle of this disastrous campaign was about to begin.

The fall
of Singapore

'The battalions crept out of their shelters to the embarkation points, then the artillery concentration began. 'On board' then 'Cast off' – the orders came from an officer a few yards away. The artillery had stopped firing now and everywhere was silent. I looked up and saw the sky was bright with stars. The second boat was launched into the channel, then the third. Then the enemy's artillery opened up.'

The writer was Kiyomoto Heida, a soldier of Matsui's 5th Division. It must have been soon after 2130 hours on 8th February that his unit embarked, for an hour later the Australians saw the landing craft approaching, and before long the whole coast from Tanjong Buloh to Tanjong Marai was under attack. Though there was a heavy fire coming down on them from both guns and mortars, the Australians of 22nd Brigade, strung out over eight miles of coastline, opened a steady fire. But the night was dark and it was only when they had set some of the craft on fire that they could see very much. For the most part they were merely aiming at black shapes, or pointing their rifles and Bren guns towards the sound of the outboard motors. The machine gunners slowly traversed their weapons but they too were firing blind and eventually used up all their ammunition. Where the hell, the troops were crying, were the searchlights? The plan, so they had been told, was that the moment the landing craft were spotted batteries of searchlights would be switched on. But what they could not know was that all the lines had been cut hours ago, so no orders reached the units concerned. It might be argued that if they had any sense at all the searchlight crews would have switched on without waiting for orders. But in fact it had been impressed on them that on no account must they use their own initiative. Brigadier Taylor (commander of 22nd Brigade) was worried apparently that the lights might be shot out before the boats arrived.

The signal lines running back to the gunners were cut also, and it was only when the Australian infantry began sending up distress rockets that any guns opened fire. But they were too little and too late. The Japanese had already begun landing.

The whole action was a tragedy and, like those on the Peninsula, it stemmed from lack of imagination and bad planning. Obviously, with a heavy bombardment there was a risk that lines would be cut, and the decision as to when the searchlights should be switched on, and artillery support was needed, should have been left to the forward infantry commander on the beaches. With the Strait less than a mile wide, which meant a run lasting ten minutes, or at the most a quarter of an hour, by the powered assault craft, there was not a second to lose. The lights should have gone on and the shells come down the moment the machine guns opened up. As it was, the Australians destroyed the first wave of assault craft and inflicted heavy casualties on the second. Soon the Japanese could see where the defended localities were sited, and steer between them. Even so many of the craft only succeeded in reaching the shore after two or three attempts. Once this happened the men dashed inland, then came round the back of the Australian defence posts. Some of these had expended all their ammunition, and so there was hand to hand fighting in the mangrove swamps, the infantry defending themselves with their bayonets. Many of the posts were overwhelmed and when this happened gaps appeared through which the next wave of assault craft came in unopposed. Steadily the weight of the assault built up, and collecting their units together, the Japanese commanders, who had compasses strapped to their wrists, led their men south towards Ama Leng. Meanwhile, the Australians who still survived tried to make their way back, and one of them, Kenneth Attiwill, who served through the whole campaign, has given a vivid picture of their plight:

Singapore: the air raids increase, the panic grows

'Groups of men became separated from their comrades in the bewildering darkness. Others lost their way. Many died. Some straggled back as far as Bukit Timah. Others even reached Singapore City, and long before they could be picked up, reorganised and sent back, the disorganisation was complete. The effect of the withdrawal was to dislocate the whole brigade area, and by ten o'clock on the morning of the 9th – less than twelve hours after the assault had been sighted – the 22nd Australian Brigade, on whose fighting power had rested the defence of the north-western area of the Island, was no longer a cohesive fighting force.'

It was midnight before Percival obtained any picture of what was happening and learned that his forecast that the assault would not be launched for several days had proved wildly inaccurate. Bennett, he also learned, had given Brigadier Taylor such reserves as he possessed for a counterattack at first light. The remaining aircraft on the island, ten Hurricanes and four obsolete Swordfish, were also ordered to attack the enemy landing areas at first light. They took off soon after 0600 hours to find a fleet of no less than eighty-four enemy aircraft approaching the island. These they intercepted, and in two dog fights shot down several of them.

Some hours before this happened the Japanese assault troops had reached the Australian positions near Ama Keng, which covered the approach to Tengah Airfield, two miles to the south. For a while the Australians held their positions and even put in a successful counterattack, but inevitably the Japanese were soon moving round the flanks, and it was necessary to retreat. The confusion in 22nd Brigade increased and Taylor decided that the only hope was to pull right back to the Jorong Road. Within six hours of landing the Japanese had succeeded in biting off most of the Western Area. When

Below: Singapore: the pillar proved no protection. **Below right:** Cars like all war material must be denied to the enemy

daylight came their advance would continue.

Before noon on the 9th, in fact, Yamashita's staff reported to him that all the infantry of 5th and 18th Divisions were across the Strait, with several of their artillery units. Now it was time for the Imperial Guards Division to land behind 5th Division but Nishimura hung back. The Guards felt they had lost face during the Muar River battle, and in a blind fury had beheaded 200 wounded left behind by the Australian and Indian brigades, who had been forced to take to the jungle and cut their way south. During this battle the commander of Yamashita's old regiment, 3rd Guards Regiment, had been wounded and Yamashita chose his replacement. Nishimura was incensed, convinced that his own prerogative had been infringed, and decided to make things as awkward for Yamashita as he possibly could. First he kept protesting that his division was being held back from the battle. Then, when orders to advance arrived, began questioning them. Yamashita wrote later: 'I ordered the Imperial Guards to cross the Strait. Then their commander asked for further orders from me. I received a message from him that his troops were hesitating to cross because of oil flames on the surface of the water. It looked to me as if he was still upset about not being able to lead the attack. I ordered him to do his duty'. Even then Nishimura did not budge and sent a young staff officer to argue with Yamashita. The latter had heard enough, and snapped at him: 'Go back to your divisional commander. Tell him the Imperial Guards Division can do as it likes in this battle'. The implied insult here was that the Imperial Guards Division was of no great importance and victory would be won without it. Enraged, Nishimura gave orders to advance.

After dark on the 9th Yamashita crossed to the island with his staff aboard a small barge. It was so crowded that the officers had to stand upright, holding each other by the shoulder. As they scrambled ashore, Colonel Tsuji felt something move under his feet and switched on his torch. There roped on the ground in

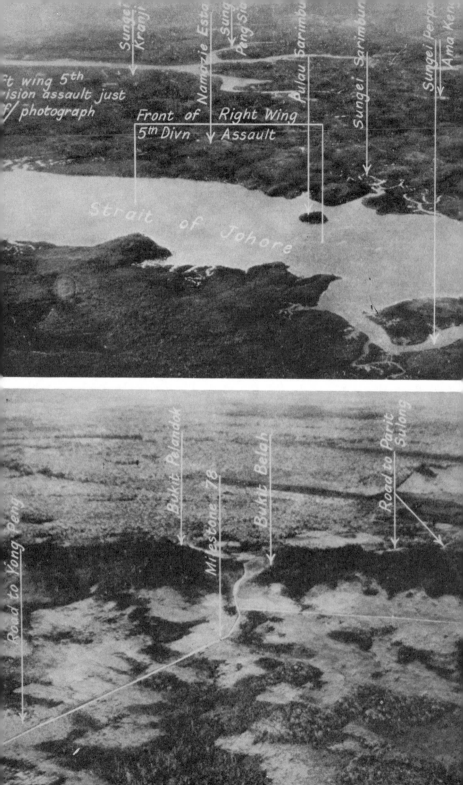

The ships leave Singapore, but some did not get far: the *Emperor of Asia* on fire following air attack

rows were British and Australian prisoners captured in the first assault, and the Japanese were now walking over them. The symbolism was too startling to be missed.

By now Gordon Bennett had been able to stabilise the situation in the Western Area, though, as he must have been aware, the Japanese were now bringing their tanks across to the Island and soon the pressure would increase considerably. However, the Jurong line was now occupied, a high ridge running for about three miles between the sources of the Kranji and Jurong rivers. Even though there was no wire and no mine fields had been laid or tank ditches dug, it was a naturally strong position. If held by resolute troops it could hold out for days.

Viewing the situation, Percival had to decide what to do if the Japanese broke through towards Bukit Timah, which lay only five miles to the north-west of Singapore City. What should

he do? Retreat to the eastern end of the island? Or form a perimeter defence line around the City? He decided to do the latter, because otherwise it would be necessary to abandon the main supply dumps and hospitals. Also it was necessary to hold on to the reservoirs supplying the town with water. During the evening of the 9th he gave his plan verbally to Heath and Simmons (commanding Southern Area) and after midnight issued it as a secret instruction for all senior commanders and their staffs. Again there was bungling, for Bennett issued an operation order based on the instructions to his brigadiers, allotting them their positions on the perimeter. Reading this, Brigadier Maxwell, commanding 27th Australian Brigade, decided that he must withdraw at once and did so without advising Gordon Bennett. Brigadier Taylor, holding the central position on the Jurong line also imagined that he had been given an order to withdraw – with the result that the Jurong line was abandoned and all hope of holding the Japanese in the west of the

Island was lost.

Such was the situation when Wavell arrived on the 10th for his last visit to the island. Visiting Gordon Bennett's headquarters with Percival, he ordered that a counterattack should be launched immediately. He had little faith, however, that it would succeed and on his return to Java signalled Churchill:

'Battle for Singapore is not going well. Japanese with their usual infiltration tactics are getting on much more rapidly than they should in the west of Island . . . Morale of some troops is not good and none is as high as I should like to see . . . The chief troubles are a lack of sufficient training in some of the reinforcing troops and an inferiority complex which bold and skilful Japanese tactics and their command of the air have caused. Everything possible is being done to produce more offensive spirit and optimistic outlook. But I cannot pretend that these efforts have been entirely successful up to date. I have given the most categorical orders that there is to be no thought of surrender and that all troops are to continue fighting to the end.'

The situation for the British continued to deteriorate, and by the afternoon of the 10th, when the Japanese medium tanks had arrived, the chaos grew worse. The Indian troops covering the hills at Bukit Timah were scattered, and that night only the Argyll and Sutherland Highlanders stood between the enemy columns and the vital Bukit Timah depots. With all the trucks and cars they could find and a few anti-tank mines, they hurriedly threw up a road block. When the Japanese column arrived about 2230 hours the leading tank was knocked out, but now came a force of no less than fifty tanks supported by infantry and these forced the Argylls to withdraw east of the road. By midnight the Japanese were controlling the vital road junction, so cutting the Allied communication from north to south.

By the morning of the 13th the Allied forces were back on a twenty-eight mile perimeter covering Singapore City. There was not much farther to go.

The city by now was in a state of complete chaos, its population doubled by 500,000 refugees. Overhead hung a thick pall of smoke from the burning oil tanks. Through the streets which were choked with abandoned vehicles, wandered troops without officers or orders. Sometimes a column would hang around for hours, having lost its way. In doorways deserters sprawled and other staggered around drunk, having looted liquor shops. Inevitably there were fights and drunken brawls. Looting by now was on a vast scale. Thousands of cigarette packets littered the pavements and children wobbled around on bicycles far too big for them. Deserters drove cars from the showrooms and careered round wildly till they were smashed up. The food shops were looted, too, and women and children could be seen hurrying along with dressed chickens, sacks full of tinned fruit, or flour or rice. The cinemas were crowded, chiefly with troops. Every hour or so there would be another air raid and the bombs could be heard exploding on the houses. People would start running out to nowhere in particular; with no shelters yet built there was nowhere to run to. All over the city fires were burning but few people took any notice. They were doomed and they knew there was nothing they could do about it.

Though the battle was going swiftly, it was still not swift enough for Yamashita. His Chief Supply Officer, Colonel Ikatini, had warned him that his army was so short of petrol and artillery ammunition that a long siege was out of the question. The line of communications from Japan to Singapore and from Singora to Singapore had broken down. What was to be done? Should he maintain the momentume of the assault, hoping that Percival would surrender? Or call a halt and wait till Southern Army bestirred itself and sent more supplies? Against the first course was Yamashita's fear that Percival would retreat into the city and fight on street by street. Such a move would have presented appalling problems for, apart from the supply problem, Yamashita's army would be outnumbered – and street fighting swallows up troops in vast numbers. But it was the first course that Yamashita chose, for he had shrewdly summed up Percival's character and realised the utter demoralisation of the Allied forces. Later he wrote:

'My attack on Singapore was a bluff, a bluff that worked. I had 30,000 men and was outnumbered by more than three to one. I knew that if I had to fight long for Singapore I would be beaten. That is why the surrender had to be at once. I was very frightened all the time that the British would discover our numerical weakness and lack of supplies and force me into disastrous street fighting.'

So the guns were ordered to go on firing as if their ammunition would last forever. And meanwhile the aircraft hammered away at the airfields and the tanks kept scattering the tired infantry. The pressure was maintained right round the clock.

In London news of the worsening situation had been received with incredulity and utter dismay. Even after the disasters of the last three years, and especially those since Japan entered the war, there was still a rooted belief that a miracle must happen. That somehow Singapore must save itself. The myth was so strong it withstood the impact of even the hardest facts. On 10th February Churchill had signalled Wavell:

'I think you ought to realise how we view the situation in Singapore. It was reported to the Cabinet that Percival has over 100,000 men, of whom 33,000 are British and 17,000 Australian. It is doubtful if the Japanese have as many in the whole Malay peninsula . . . In these circumstances the defenders must greatly outnumber Japanese forces who have crossed the straits, and in a well-contested battle should destroy them. There must at this stage be no thought of saving the troops or sparing the civilian population. The battle must be fought to the bitter end at all costs . . . Commanders and senior officers should die with their troops. The honour of the British Empire and of the British Army is at stake. I rely on you to show no mercy to weakness in any form.'

In his reply, Wavell was pessimistic. Though Percival had not so many troops as Churchill imagined, he said, 'He should have . . . quite enough to deal with enemy who have landed if the troops can be made to act with sufficient vigour and determination.' He also gave the news that on returning from Singapore he had fallen from the quay in the dark and had broken two small bones in his back. He would be crippled for the next few weeks. It was from hospital that Wavell signalled Percival on the 13th:

'You must fight it out to the end as you are doing. But when everything humanly possible has been done some bold and determined personnel may be able to escape by small craft and find their way south to Sumatra and the islands.'

The same day Percival signalled to Wavell:

'Enemy now within 5,000 yards of sea-front, which brings whole of Singapore town within field artillery range. We are also in danger of being driven off water and food supplies. In opinion of commanders troops already committed are too exhausted either to withstand strong attack or launch counterattack . . . In these conditions it is unlikely that resistance can last more than a day or two . . . There must come a stage when in the interests of the troops and civilian population further bloodshed will serve no useful purpose. Your instructions of February 10 are being carried out, but in above circumstances would you consider giving me wider discretion powers?'

The formal language did not obscure the reality of Percival's plea: he wanted to surrender. But Wavell would not play, and signalled back on the 14th:

'You must continue to inflict maximum damage on enemy for as long as possible by house-to-house fighting if necessary. Your action in tying down enemy and inflicting casualties may have vital influence in other theatres. Fully appreciate your situation, but continued action essential.'

Meanwhile Churchill had been reviewing the situation and came to the conclusion that now 'it was certain all was lost at Singapore, it would be wrong to enforce needless slaughter.' So the same day he signalled Wavell:

'You are of course sole judge of the moment when no further result can be gained at Singapore, and should

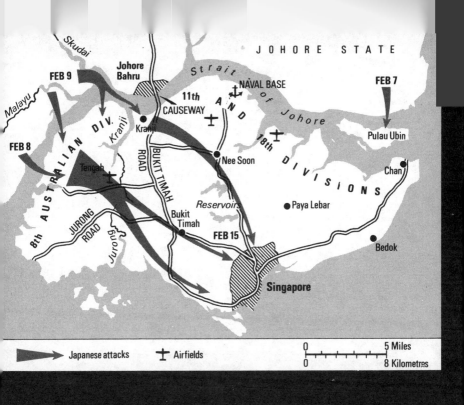

JOHORE STATE

FEB 9

Skudai

Malayu

Johore
Bahru

FEB 7

Strait

AND

of

11th
CAUSEWAY

NAVAL BASE

Johore

FEB 8

8th AUSTRALIAN DIV.

Kranji

Kranji

Pulau Ubin

18th

ROAD

Tengah

Nee Soon

DIVISIONS

Chan

BUKIT TIMAH

Paya Lebar

Reservoirs

JURONG ROAD

Bukit
Timah

FEB 15

Bedok

Jurong

Singapore

Japanese attacks   ✈ Airfields

0   5 Miles
0   8 Kilometres

Percival walks to meet his conqueror under a white flag

instruct Percival accordingly.'

The following day Wavell signalled Percival, advising him of the change in the situation:

'So long as you are in position to inflict losses and damage to enemy and your troops are physically capable of doing so you must fight on. Time gained and damage to enemy are of vital importance at this crisis. When you are fully satisfied that this is no longer possible I give you dis-

cretion to cease resistance . . . Whatever happens I thank you and al troops for gallant efforts of last fev days.'

Percival received this signal witl relief for his problems in Singapor were mounting rapidly. The onl; water supplies reaching the city cam from a pumping station at Woodleigh which was now barely half a mil from the Japanese forward positions Now, owing to broken mains, two thirds of this supply was running t waste, and in some parts of the cit; no water was available at all. Briga

dier Simson and parties of Royal Engineers tried valiantly to repair the mains and keep supplies moving but it was quite hopeless. Soon it was evident that the danger of a typhoid epidemic was increasing, for bodies had been reported in the reservoirs and Asians were drinking contaminated supplies. At 10am on Saturday the 14th Simson had to tell Percival that a complete failure of the water supply seemed likely within forty-eight hours. Percival's reaction was to call in the Municipal Engineer, and after a brief conference he announced: 'While there's water we fight on.'

To Shenton Thomas, the governor, however, the danger of an epidemic was overriding and he signalled the Colonial Office in London to give them the situation as he saw it:

'General Officer Commanding informs me that Singapore City is now invested. There are now one million people within radius of three miles. Water-supplies very badly damaged and unlikely to last more than twenty-four hours. Many dead lying in the streets and burial impossible.

After the surrender. *Left:* British troops are disarmed by the Japanese.
Above: Japanese infantry march into Raffles Place

We are faced with total deprivation of water, which must result in pestilence. I have felt that it is my duty to bring this to notice of General Officer Commanding.'

Shenton Thomas had kept up the pretence of normality right to the last minute, insisting that guests to Government House should wear collars and ties and the day's menu was printed as it had always been.

On Sunday the 15th, Percival called a conference of his commanders and senior staff at Fort Canning at 0930 hours. From each one he heard a brief report of the situation and from each learned that the situation was quite hopeless. There was almost no water . . . the Army had rations for only a few days . . . the only petrol left was in the tanks of trucks. It did not take long for any last flickering ray of hope to be extinguished and after a quarter of an hour or so, as Gordon Bennett recorded, 'Silently and sadly we decided to surrender.'

Three days earlier Yamashita had dropped a note from the air addressed to 'The High Command of the British Army', which read:

'Your Excellency,

I, the High Command of the Nippon Army based on the spirit of Japanese chivalry, have the honour of presenting this note to Your Excellency advising you to surrender the whole force in Malaya.

My sincere respect is due to your army which, true to the traditional spirit of Great Britain, is bravely defending Singapore which now stands isolated and unaided. Many fierce and gallant fights have been fought by your gallant men and officers, to the honour of British warriorship. But the developments of the general war situation has already sealed the fate of Singapore, and the continuation of futile resistance would only serve to inflict direct harm and injuries to thousands of noncombatants living in the city, throwing them into further miseries and horrors of war, but also would not add anything to the honour of your army.

I expect that Your Excellency accepting my advice will give up this meaningless and desperate resistance and promptly order the entire front to cease hostilities and will despatch

145

at the same time your parliamentaire according to the procedure shown at the end of this note. If on the contrary, Your Excellency should neglect my advice and the present resistance be continued, I shall be obliged, though reluctant from humanitarian considerations, to order my army to make annihilating attacks on Singapore.

On closing this note of advice, I pay again my sincere respects to Your Excellency.

(Signed) Tomoyuki Yamashita.
1. The Parliamentaire should proceed to the Bukit Timah Road.
2. The Parliamentaire should bear a large white flag and the Union Jack.'

Yamashita had received no reply to this communication and with his ammunition stocks going down rapidly, had begun to wonder if disaster threatened him after all. Once the fighting started in the streets, it might go on endlessly, rifle against rifle, and bayonet against bayonet. Neither his tanks nor his artillery could dominate the battle as they had done up to now, and with the armies locked in close combat, even air superiority would cease to be a decisive factor. The fighting continued throughout the 13th and 14th . . . and on the morning of Sunday the 15th Yamashita went forward to Mutaguchi's headquarters, situated on the vantage point of Bukit Timah. A pall of thick smoke overlay the city, and Mutaguchi reported that enemy artillery fire had slackened. Several batteries, he believed, had been knocked out by air-strikes. Full as always of the lust for combat, Mutaguchi had been watching his troops in action by the south coast, where since dawn, he reported to Yamashita, they had advanced two miles.

At about ten o'clock, when Yamashita had returned to his own headquarters, a patrol sent out from Mutaguchi's division reported that a flag had gone up among the trees ahead. An officer was called to verify the report, and he then telephoned Mutaguchi that a white flag had also gone up on the broadcasting studios. Later a car approached along the Bukit

15th February 1942: Percival surrenders to Yamashita

Timah Road under a flag of truce, and Lieutenant-Colonel Sugita, an Intelligence Officer on Yamashita's headquarters went forward to meet it.

In the car was Brigadier Newbiggin, Percival's Chief Administrative Officer, and Hugh Fraser, the Acting Colonial Secretary, and before they could reach the Japanese lines they ran up against a mine field. It was therefore necessary to abandon the car and go ahead on foot, carrying the flag of truce. Eventually some Japanese troops came out of the rubber plantations their guns at the ready. Finally realising what the white flag portended, they asked the British to line up for photographs. For a while there was a good deal of jostling as each soldier tried to get into the picture then choose a vantage point to take his own.

At 1400 hours Sugita and a junior officer arrived, to whom Newbiggin gave a letter from Percival suggesting that there should be a cease-fire at 1600 hours to allow the two commanders to discuss the terms of surrender. Yamashita's instructions to Sugita, however, admitted no discussions; he would not cease fire until Percival had signed a document of surrender. As he wrote later: I prepared myself against being deceived and ordered the British com-

The victor: Yamashita walks through Singapore with his staff

mander to come in person.' The rendezvous was laid down at the Ford Factory at Bukit Timah and here Percival arrived at 1715 hours with two staff officers and an interpeter. Yamashita arrived a few minutes later and, after introductions had been effected by his interpreter, Hishikari, the commanders sat down facing each other under the eye of news photographers and news cameramen. According to the official Japanese account of the meeting, the dialogue went as follows:

'Answer me briefly – Do you wish to surrender unconditionally?'

'Yes – we do.'

'Have you any Japanese prisoners of war?'

'None at all.'

'Have you any Japanese civilians?'

'No. They have all been sent to India.'

'Very well. Will you please sign this document of surrender?'

Percival read about half of it then asked:

'Will you give me until tomorrow morning?'

Yamashita replied angrily:

'If you don't sign now we shall go on fighting. All I want to know is: Do you surrender unconditionally or do you not?'

Percival went pale and began talking to the interpreter in a low voice but Yamashita interrupted him, pointed his finger and shouted: 'Yes or No?'

Percival glanced towards the interpreter then said: 'Yes.'

'Very well then. We shall cease hostilities at 10pm Japanese time.'

Having signed, Percival requested that Japanese forces should not enter the city till the following morning, as he needed time to communicate the surrender to outlying commanders and to the civilian population. After Yamashita agreed, the following exchange took place:

'What about the lives of the civilians, and the British, Indian and Australian troops? Will you guarantee them?'

'Yes. You may be easy about that. I can guarantee them absolutely.'

With this the meeting came to an end. Yamashita's adjutant wrote:

'The meeting between the two commanders ended at 1900 hours when the enemy accepted unconditional surrender. Yamashita stood up and again shook hands with the enemy commander. He was surrounded by cameramen and war reporters. He told me afterwards that he wanted to say a few kind words to Percival while he was shaking hands with him, as he looked so pale and thin and ill. But he could not say anything as he did not speak English and realised how difficult it is to convey heartfelt sympathy when the words are being interpreted by a third person.'

With the signing of the document of surrender, Yamashita gained the greatest triumph of any general in the history of the Japanese army. The great base of Singapore, with its huge natural resources, could now be held and developed for the national war effort. His campaign had lasted only seventy-three days and his total casulties were only 9,824 of whom about 3,000 were killed. And 80,000 men had laid down their arms to him.

To the Allies, and especially to Winston Churchill, the disaster was so staggering as to defy the imagination. It would be some time before its true proportions could be realised. Meanwhile Churchill's only cheer came in the form of a signal from the President of the United States, Franklyn D Roosevelt, whose army in the Philippines was to suffer the same fate as the British:

'I realise how the fall of Singapore has affected you and the British people. It gives the well-known back-seat driver a field day, but no matter how serious our setbacks have been . . . we must constantly look forward to the next moves that need to be made to hit the enemy. I hope you will be of good heart in these trying weeks, because I am very sure that you have the great confidence of the masses of the British people. I want you to know that I think of you often, and I know you will not hesitate to ask me if there is anything you think I can do . . . Do let me hear from you.'

Whether America ever had a greater president than Franklyn D Roosevelt, it is not for an Englishman to say, but certainly England never had a greater friend. Now she would need him more than ever.

Postscript and post mortem

Like every other tragedy, the loss of Malaya and Singapore provokes many questions. If 11th Division had been allowed to consolidate at Jitra, instead of being launched into the futile Matador operation. If the aircraft carrier Indomitable had not been beached in Jamaica . . . if the troops had been led by a good field commander instead of Percival . . . if the north shore of Singapore Island had been fortified . . . if the infantry had been supported by even two regiments of tanks. One could go on endlessly but to no purpose. The brutal truth is that the battle was lost years before it started. As Wavell wrote on hearing of the surrender: 'The trouble goes back a long way: climate, the atmosphere of the country (the whole of Malaya has been asleep for at least two hundred years), lack of vigour in our peacetime training, and cumbrousness of our tactics and equipment, and the real difficulty of finding an answer to the very skilful and bold tactics of the Japanese in this jungle fighting.'

Even good, trained troops are no use without equipment but it is futile to blame the British government for not sending the tanks and the aircraft. These did not exist. Such slender resources that were available had to be concentrated for the defence of the homeland, for if England fell to the Germans, all hope of recovery would be lost. So Malaya, and indeed all British possessions in the Far East including Burma, remained at the end of the queue. It is interesting to note that exactly the same situation happened in the Philippines. Even all the vast resources of the United States could not equip these territories in time to face the Japanese invasion.

So the truth is that given a Montgomery instead of a Percival, the result would have been the same in the end, even if delayed. The British army simply had not learned the art of operating in thick country and would not do so for another two years. It was March 1944 before XV Indian Corps in the Arakan showed how the Japanese tactics could be

The plight of civilians: the Japanese had many scores to settle

150

Bayonet practice

overcome, with the use of aircraft. But before these tactics could be employed, air superiority had to be wrested from the Japanese. The air, in fact, held the key to the whole situation.

Yamashita's guarantees for the safety of soldiers and civilians were not observed. Hundreds of Chinese were driven to the east coast of Singapore Island, made to dig their own graves, and then were mown down in lines. Mutaguchi's 18th Division ran amok among the wounded, and later thousands of prisoners of war were to meet their fate on 'the Death Railway'. When the *Kempei* (Tojo's Secret Police) arrived in Singapore, there were to be more arrests and killings and many people disappeared. To what extent the brutalities were the responsibility of Yamashita himself it is hard to say; the task facing him was a formidable one, and he had to ask British firemen, doctors, nurses, engineers, and sanitary workers to remain where they were until their jobs could be taken over by Japanese.

He certainly denied himself the bombast of a conqueror, and when Terauchi signalled asking when the triumphal entry into Singapore would take place his reply was: 'Twenty-fifth Army will not hold parade but funeral ceremony is fixed for 20th February'. A few days later Terauchi signalled that he would be moving into Singapore with Southern Army Headquarters and Twenty-fifth Army would have to move to Indonesia.

What was to be Yamashita's next role? Would he lead his army against Australia, as he wished, or would he head west for Burma and then India? In July he learned that the post selected for him was that of 1st Area Commander in Manchukuo, the puppet state set up by the Japanese army in Manchuria. His task would be to defend the eastern region of this country against Russia, and in the event of war, to attack the Siberian port of Vladivostock. Though a post of some importance, this could only be regarded by Yamashita as an insult. After a great victory he was to be shunted away to a remote non-operational area, where most of his time would be taken up with training troops. However, he accepted the order and made no complaint. All he wanted now was to appear before the Emperor to ask forgiveness for his part in the bloody incident of February 1936. Confident that permission would be given, he prepared a document to read before the Emperor, giving his account of the Malaya campaign. But then there came two shattering blows. First he learned that Tojo had sent orders that he was to proceed to his new command direct. And next he was informed that the Emperor had by no means forgotten the events of February 1936, and re-

used to grant an interview, either now or in the foreseeable future.

On 17th July, the conqueror of Singapore set out on the bleak journey to Manchukuo. Here he was to remain till 25th September 1944, when he received a summons to take over the Japanese forces in the Philippines, now awaiting attack from the avenging armies of General Douglas MacArthur. There is no need to trace the course of the subsequent campaign. On 1st September, when the remains of his army were trapped in the mountains of Luzon he decided that he must obey the Emperor's orders and surrender himself.

Percival had been held as a prisoner of war, first in Singapore and then on Formosa and in Manchuria, and was half-starved like most of his men. With the Japanese surrender, he received the glad news that with General Wainwright (the Americans' gallant commander on Bataan), he had been invited by MacArthur to attend the surrender ceremony in Tokyo Bay. Afterwards he went on to the Philippines, where again he was to sit

The road to Changi prison camp: it was to be a hard sentence

opposite Yamashita, but in very different circumstances. Later he wrote:

'As Yamashita entered the room I saw one eyebrow lifted and a look of surprise cross his face – but only for a moment. His face quickly resumed the sphinx-like mask common to all Japanese, and he showed no further interest.'

Later on Yamashita was tried by a United States Military Commission for 'brutal atrocities and other high crimes against the people of the United States and its allies and dependencies', chiefly committed in Manila. He was found guilty and was hanged on 23rd February 1946.

Yamashita's story has been told in detail elsewhere and there is no need to repeat it here. Sufficient to say that between the time he left Singapore and the time he died the fortunes of Japan had run full circle. After Singapore they had gone on to capture the Philippines and the East Indies, they had swept through Burma and by the summer of 1942 stood on the frontiers of India. But they went no further. The Australians outfought them in New Guinea. The Americans counterattacked in the Pacific. Then, in 1944, after Mutaguchi's 'March on Delhi' the British, who had now found two great commanders in Admiral Lord Mountbatten and General Slim, struck back and within twelve months won the greatest land victory ever achieved against Japan in her entire history. Three entire armies, the Fifteenth, Twenty-eighth and Thirty-third, were irretrievably smashed, 190,000 men lay dead on the battlefield and, before the atom bomb dropped on Hiroshima, the whole of Burma was clear of the enemy. Happily to relate the Indian troops, which Yamashita had so much despised, played a major part in this victory; properly trained and equipped they demonstrated their superiority.

But the Allied victory over Japan could not alter one thing which Singapore had demonstrated beyond all doubt. That the place of the white man in the east would never be the same again. Singapore and the Malay States would gain their freedom, just like the Philippines and Indonesia. Happily one can report that at the moment they are at peace.

Below: Humiliation: Asians watch Australian prisoners of war sweep the streets. *Right:* For many the Allies returned to Singapore almost too late: men released from Changi prison camp

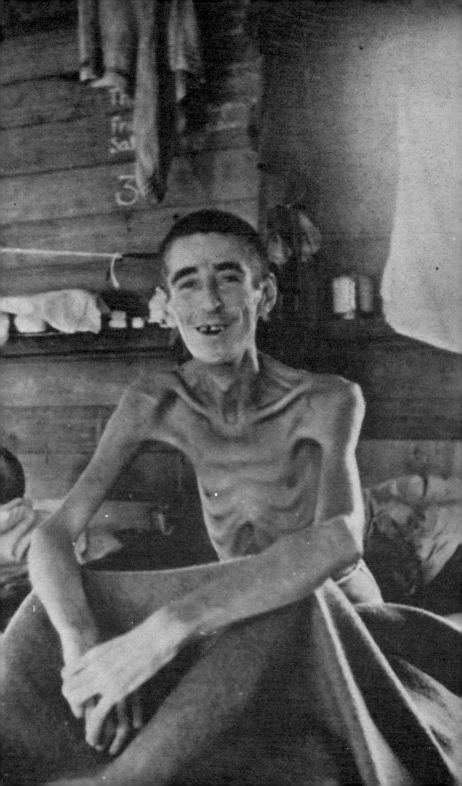

Yamashita on trial

Bibliography

Sinister Twilight Noel Barber (Collins, London)
The Second World War vol. 4 The Hinge of Fate Winston Churchill (Cassell, London)
Official War History vol. 1 The War Against Japan Major-General S Woodburn Kirby and others (HMSO, London)
Singapore James Leasor (Doubleday, New York)
The Fall of Singapore Frank Owen (Michael Joseph, London)
The War in Malaya Lieutenant-General A E Percival (Eyre and Spottiswoode London)
A Soldier Must Hang John Deane Potter (Frederick Muller, London)
Four Samurai Arthur Swinson (Hutchinson, London)
History of the Second World War vol. 2 no. 13 (Purnell & Son, London)
Singapore Colonel Masanobu Tsuji trans. Margaret E Lake (Constable, London)
History of the Pacific War vol. 3 Historical Research Group (Toyokeizaishinposha, Tokyo)

Ballantine's Illustrated History of World War II is an entirely new and exciting venture in paperback publishing. Never before has the attempt been made to explore in depth so gigantic and world-shaking an event as World War II, and then to present the results to the public in the form of short, crisply but authentically-written narratives, richly illustrated *throughout the text* with photographs, maps and diagrams.

Already the first twenty books in this magnificent series are available. They are . . .

D-Day by R W Thompson
(Battle book, No 1)

Afrika Korps by Kenneth Macksey
(Campaign book, No 1)

Their Finest Hour by Edward Bishop
(Battle book, No 2)

U-boat by David Mason
(Weapons book, No 1)

Stalingrad by Geoffrey Jukes
(Battle book, No 3)

Panzer Division by Kenneth Macksey
(Weapons book, No 2)

Aircraft Carrier by Donald Macintyre
(Weapons book, No 3)

Bastogne by Peter Elstob
(Battle book, No 4)

ME109 by Martin Caidin
(Weapons book, No 4)

The Siege of Leningrad by Alan Wykes
(Battle book, No 5)

The Raiders by Arthur Swinson
(Campaign book, No 2)

Battle for Berlin by Earl Ziemke
(Battle book, No 6)

Sicily by Martin Blumenson
(Campaign book, No 3)

Kursk by Geoffrey Jukes
(Battle book, No 7)

Tarawa by Henry I Shaw
(Battle book, No 8)

Breakout from Normandy by David Mason
(Campaign book, No 4)

German Secret Weapons by Brian Ford
(Weapons book, No 5)

Spitfire by John Vader
(Weapons book, No 6)

Commando by Peter Young
(Weapons book, No 7)

Operation Market Garden (Arnhem) by
Anthony Farrar-Hockley (Battle book, No 9)

Further titles include . . .

Pearl Harbor by A J Barker
(Battle book, No 10)

SS and Gestapo by Roger Manvell
(Weapons book, No 8)

Leyte Gulf by Donald Macintyre
(Battle book, No 11)

Okinawa by Benis M Franks
(Battle book, No 12)

Zero Fighter by Martin Caidin
(Weapons book, No 9)

The Fall of Singapore by Arthur Swinson
(Campaign book, No 5)

The Airborne by Charles MacDonald
(Weapons book, No 10)

Birth and Death of the Luftwaffe
by Alfred Price
(Weapons book, No 11)

The Fall of France by John Williams
(Campaign book, No 6)

The Defence of Moscow
by Geoffrey Jukes
(Campaign book, No 7)

The Nuremberg Rallies by Alan Wykes
(Campaign book, No 8)

The Gun by Ian V Hogg
(Weapons book, No 12)

The Bombing of Europe by
Noble Frankland
(Campaign book, No 9)

The Fall of Japan by Alvin D Coox
(Campaign book, No 10)

The B29 by Carl Berger
(Weapons book, No 13)

Motor Torpedo Boat by Bryan Cooper
(Weapons book, No 14)

**Pacific Hawk: Kittihawks in the South
Pacific** by John Vader
(Weapons book, No 15)

The Raid on St. Nazaire by David Mason
(Battle book, No 13)

Battle of Anzio by Christopher Hibbert
(Battle book, No 14)

The Waffen SS by John Keegan
(Weapons book, No 16)

The Blitz on London by Constantine
FitzGibbon (Battle book, No 15)

Allied Armour by Kenneth Macksey
(Weapons book, No 17)

The Battle of the Reichswald
by Peter Elstob (Battle book, No 16)

Normandy Bridgehead by H Essame
(Campaign book, No 11)

Ballantine Books is proud to present this series.

Code: Battle books: orange band. Campaign books: yellow ochre band.
Weapons books: blue band.

The colony paid in full for Britain's incredible
failure to recognise the growing Japanese
menace. One route into Singapore — through th
jungle — was 'impossible' for an invading arm
... but through the jungle they came. And a
humiliating, bloody retreat left the civilians to
the harrowing occupation.

Cover printed in

Ballantine's Illustrated
History of World War II **BB** campaign
book, No 5